FUN WITH ROPES AND SPARS

FUN WITH ROPES AND SPARS

MORE PIONEERING PROJECTS

by

JOHN THURMAN

Camp Chief, Gilwell Park

Illustrated by Kenneth Brookes and John Sweet

Publication Approved
by
THE BOY SCOUTS ASSOCIATION

C. ARTHUR PEARSON, LTD.
TOWER HOUSE, SOUTHAMPTON STREET,
LONDON, W.C.2

To

MY WIFE

*Who always lets me play
at Pioneering, instead of
mending the latch on the gate*

Made and Printed in Great Britain by Butler & Tanner Ltd., Frome and London

CONTENTS

CONTENTS

AUTHOR'S NOTE

A<small>T</small> odd places in this book, under the heading " Try These Ideas ", I offer you ideas, many of which I hope you will try out. I am quite deliberately not telling you how they can be done but I will tell you that they all have been done and they do add to our knowledge of the use of blocks, spars, ropes, and the rest. They are good fun and many of them can be tackled indoors or out-of-doors as well as in light or heavy material.

J. T.

I

SETTING ABOUT THE JOB

CHAPTER II of *Pioneering Projects* is headed "How to Build Anything—or—Stand Back, Scouter!" In case you have not read that book and because I think it is important, I am going to repeat here some of that chapter and, indeed, add to it. First and foremost, let us deal with that sub-heading "Stand Back, Scouter!" One of the eternal problems of Scouting is that it is designed for boys and yet it appeals to men, but the man's job is to stand back and let the Scouts train themselves so far as is reasonable. This demands a great deal of self-discipline, a very unselfish attitude, and, in addition, a clear understanding that the means, in this case pioneering, doesn't happen to be the end. I hope all the things we do in Scouting are useful in themselves, but the plain fact in life as it is today and likely to be in the foreseeable future is that comparatively few of us have to make rafts, rustic bridges, and aerial runways, to say nothing of the more extravagant fantasies I have already presented to you and shall no doubt add to in the course of this book.

Certainly, knowing how to tie a knot, how to make a good lashing, and how to fix one thing to another, can be very useful but, so far as the Scouter is concerned, it is not the practical use of the idea that matters so much as the opportunity it provides for his Scouts to go into action, to learn their own personal strengths and weaknesses and gradually to develop those qualities of character which good, practical Scouting can and does develop.

In that chapter to which I have referred I mentioned six particular questions which I think we have to answer before we set out upon the task of building anything, and in *Pioneering Projects* I used the questions throughout. This time, however, for a change, I thought I would refer to the questions here and remind you that they need answering in regard to each individual

[7]

project, but I shall not deal with them in detail in quite the same way as previously. Well, here they are again, familiar to some of you, old friends, I hope, and not boring companions ; they really do matter tremendously and I hope you will read them and think about them until you thoroughly know them.

Question 1.—" What have we to do ? " I suppose that at first sight this seems to be an unnecessary question. If we are going to make a bridge then the short answer is that we are going to make a bridge but, like most short answers, it is a little incomplete. All kinds of secondary questions arise immediately ; " What sort of bridge ? " " Is the particular bridge we have in mind suitable for our purpose ? " " Is it suitable to the place where we are going to build it or is there a better bridge ? " " Are we building it because we have never built it before—and that is not a bad reason for doing something—or are we going to build it because we have often built it before and we know we can do it ? " The latter is not a good reason ; Scouting and pioneering are supposed to be adventurous and this must mean the willingness to tackle new ideas and not just to remain faithful to the old ones. In short, when we begin to think about this question, all kinds of queries arise, I hope, in your mind as they certainly do in mine, and doubts arise, both practical and theoretical, which I want to help you to resolve. Adventure is not foolhardiness. Nearly always, a man who does something supremely worthwhile in an emergency is the man who has experienced something similar previously : he may have had practice in a completely artificial setting but he is disciplined and trained so that his mind works quickly and his actions are correct when the need arises. Inspiration is not something which suddenly hits you when you need it. Nearly always it comes to the people who have used their heads or, rather, what is inside them to think and plan and it comes only to those who take the trouble to use their own powers of imagination.

When we try to answer this first question all sorts of thoughts and ideas ought to crowd into our heads. The Patrol in Council, the Troop Court of Honour, or the Scouters' Council, may ponder for ten minutes over a proposed project to see if they can satisfactorily answer the question, " What have we to do ? "

Question 2.—" What do we need to achieve it ? " This really resolves itself into two parts : " What kind of gear are we going to need ? " and " Where are we going to build it ? " The second part I deal with in my answer to Question 3. One of the things I did not say in *Pioneering Projects* and was rather taken to task about by an old friend was a reference to pioneering equipment owned and looked after centrally by a Scout District. Well, perhaps this is the place to remedy my omission.

Of course it is a good thing for a District to have a central store of spars and heavy ropes and the like, and what an excellent job this is for a Rover Scout ; he could be in charge of it, maintain and add to it, and encourage its use. It would, of course, detract from the idea if all the Troops in the District relied solely on the central store and never possessed so much as a rope of their own.

Districts vary considerably in the matter of finance, opportunities for storing equipment, and in many other ways. I don't care much for generalisation but I think this question of District pioneering equipment is one which the Commissioner and the Scouters concerned should discuss very fully. They should discuss whether they are going to have it, what they are going to have, where it is to be kept, who is going to look after it, and what are the terms of its use. Anyway, it is an idea and one that is working well in some places. Perhaps in your District it will be the answer to your problems, so think about it.

On equipment generally I have little to say. Remember that with ropes and spars particularly it pays to get the best you can afford ; they will give the best results, will last longer and, in the long run, will prove to be the cheapest, but there are all kinds of oddments which we need for pioneering which are not expensive ; such things as oil drums, odd lengths of sisal, old guy ropes ; the sides of a tent which is too old to keep out the rain might make a sail for a raft. It is impossible to make a complete list but, except for cast iron which is too heavy for our sort of pioneering, there are very few old articles which I have seen and could not find a use for in pioneering.

Note that I said " old " and not " decayed ". A cart wheel riddled with dry rot is no use to the cart or to Scouting. A thing which is old can still be good and, whilst it is right and a joy to improvise, it is a lot of nonsense to think that you can build a bridge or a raft with a lot of decayed junk which is quite unsafe and may prove dangerous.

I would like to add a word on this question of improvisation. There are some things that you cannot improvise with satisfaction or with safety, and we should not try to do so, but there are many occasions when something less than the best will satisfy. Again, it is not possible to make a list as it would vary from project to project, but to err on the side of reasonable safety does not mean that one lacks adventure. Because I want pioneering to be enjoyed, and it will not be enjoyed if the first time a strain is put on the bridge the whole thing collapses, I repeat, make sure your equipment is safe.

I was in Australia a year or two ago and I heard a most delightful description of a bridge which had collapsed. A Patrol of fellows on a Training Course had worked hard all morning with some rather inadequate equipment, trying to bridge a chasm in the rock. The chasm did not lend itself to the particular type of bridge they were building and the finished article was a very ramshackle affair. The Patrol Leader was bludgeoned into trying the bridge and the whole thing subsided gently but very definitely into the small but wet stream at the bottom of the gulley. The P.L. recovered his equilibrium very quickly and, dripping wet, went up to the Scouter in charge, saluted and said, " Bridge prematurely dismantled, sir." A pleasing way, I thought, of underlining the obvious !

We shall refer quite a lot to gear as the book proceeds and, as before, I am going to head chapters where necessary with a list of what I think is needed, but please check the list for yourself before you start on the job because it may be that there will be a few undeliberate mistakes ; I will try to avoid them, but it is easy for a mistake to creep in. If an error does occur I shall, of course, blame the printer, but it will not make much difference to you as to whether it is my fault or the fault of the printer if you set out with a list of equipment which you have not checked and find you are missing some vital part. In pioneering, as in many other pursuits, at some stage you must learn to rely on yourself.

Question 3 is " Where are we going to build it ? " I have really dealt with this already in *Pioneering Projects*. Do you remember that I said you should check the type of soil for hold-fasts ? It is no use expecting a picket to hold in a bed of sand. Do you remember that I warned you against the deceptive top spit of the world ? Find out what is underneath before you decide to build on just that spot. There is an extra point I would make here. If you are going to try out the ideas I suggest in this book then you will have to find sites other than the normal ones on which to carry out some of the projects, but don't be daunted by that ; your share in the adventure is the finding of a place where it is worthwhile to have a shot at what is suggested.

Question 4.—" How long have we got ? " Heaven knows how I can answer this for you, but it is a question which must be answered. When you see Scouts set out on a pioneering project they seem to fall into two groups, those who think it is essential to build a bridge in less than three minutes—which would be difficult for most of us—and those who clearly are going to grow old in the pioneering service and will no doubt be invested as Rovers or possibly apply to join the Old Scout Branch when the job is completed. It really is a good thing to set yourself a time limit and to work to it, and it is a good idea to set a time limit a little less than you think you really need. I am sure a Patrol pulls best when it is rather up against it. You must, of course, make the project possible but not too easy ; to ask the impossible never achieves anything. I know B.-P. said we must learn to take the " im " out of impossible, but he was a realist and what he meant was that we should set our standards high and bring within our compass things which previously had seemed impossible.

[11]

So we come to the *fifth question*, " Who is going to do what, and in what order ? " or, more simply, " How are we going to do it ? " Well, we've come full circle and are back to the Patrol in Council or the Court of Honour. Sit down with the drawing of the project, check the gear, think about the site, and spend a few minutes deciding how the whole thing is to be tackled. I hope that during the book I will be able to advise you in individual cases, but I shall leave a lot unsaid because I do not want this book to be a textbook. I want the book to prod you into action and make Scouts do things for themselves.

So to the final question, " Have we cleared up ? " Well, have you ? Really ? Lashings counted ; pegs all there ? That bit of sisal you pushed into a hole ?

Lastly for this chapter, another word for the Scouter, and the P.L. might read it too : do please see that the Scouts enjoy themselves. I realise that you cannot force people to enjoy themselves but you can lead them to try to enjoy themselves. If you are for ever nagging and poking and prying into every lashing they will get fed up with the job and with you. If you are for ever saying the obvious it will become very wearisome. Let them find out from their errors. If a thing really does seem to be dangerous then say a few words, but keep your homily short and don't give a lecture.

The general tendency will be to try a thing before it is ready, well, let them but if they want you to try it before it is ready it is a different matter and I must leave that to your discretion. I regard a change of clothes as a necessity for the Scouter when he is concerned with pioneering ; walking home in a borrowed pair of shorts, especially if you are normal size and your Scouts are small, is liable to be misunderstood as well as being uncomfortable.

So much for the preliminaries ; now let's get on with the job.

2

THE USE OF MODELS

SOMETIMES opportunity for doing full-scale pioneering out-of-doors is limited and that is one reason why I think models have their place in pioneering training, but another and perhaps more significant reason is that it is often difficult to visualise and to cope with the practical problems of a full-scale job. A great many possible errors can be, as it were, anticipated and thus overcome by making working models of the things we are eventually going to make full size. The model will also encourage good handicraft, an activity about which B.-P., the Founder, was very keen and which all too often is left just as one of those things we mean to do one day but somehow never get round to doing.

There is another reason why I would advocate the model, and that is for the Scout or the Troop that is handicapped in some physical way. Many years ago I helped to run a Troop of crippled boys in an orthopædic hospital and very few of them could take part in real pioneering but most of them were able to make models and I believe they had as much thrill out of models, handling them, and visualising them full size as they would have done in trying to make the actual things. Fortunately, the number of handicapped boys is only a small proportion of the total strength of the Movement, but those of us who are fit are apt to overlook them. I do want to suggest that the older Scout and the Rover Scout think over this question of models and see if they can help to bring pioneering into the life of a Handicapped Troop or an individual Scout. If you do this you will find that their standard in model-making is remarkably high ; they need the lead, the encouragement, and the materials.

I do not pretend to be an expert model-maker myself, but I can tell you the sort of things you are going to need. This is not a complete list but is enough to start with.

Dowelling, masses of it, for the spars. You can make it yourself on a lathe or buy it of varying thicknesses, or, of course, you can collect twigs, but in any case you are going to need a lot of it.

I ought to add that there is no use in making models unless you make them approximately to scale and for most of the projects in this book and in *Pioneering Projects* if you work to a scale of about one-sixteenth you will have a manageable model and one which is really effective for demonstration purposes. If you use a larger scale the model is apt to seem almost as big as the actual thing and to become rather a nuisance around the house, and if you use a smaller scale you will need to be very much more expert as the work becomes very intricate and may become so finicky that you will not see the snags of the full-scale article. So I suggest a scale of one-sixteenth.

Then you are going to need cord of varying thicknesses. The cord and the spars are your two main components.

You will also require a base board, because if you are going to do a real job you will have to construct a model of the river you are going to bridge or sail down with a raft as well as the actual bridge or raft itself, and for that you are going to need a good solid base board about ¾ inch thick. On it, using, I suggest, plaster of paris you will construct the banks into which you will put any natural features such as trees and any unnatural features such as pickets which the job may require. The disadvantage of plaster is its weight. Plasticine will do but it tends to change its shape when prodded, but there are a number of modelling waxes on the market today which will do very well.

Then you need all the oddments ; oil drums I think you must make yourself from tin or wood suitably painted ; canvas ; blocks, the hardest of all to make ; you can purchase them but I hope you won't because they are very expensive and if you are keen on model-making you will take great pride in making these intricate things yourself. Then you are going to need a tool box which need not contain a great deal : a small putty knife, two or three pen knives, a set of small chisels, scissors, glue, pins, wire, pliers ; I think that is enough to start with, but you will no doubt have some pet tool of your own which you would not be happy without.

I have included in the photographic inset between pages 104 and 105 photographs of models which have been made, and incidentally all made by Scouts, and you will see how realistic they are, and you will see too, I hope, that they are all working models. I think it is very important that they should embody exactly the same principles for any moving parts as the full-scale article itself.

* * * * *

TRY THESE IDEAS

1. Make a weighing machine capable of weighing accurately from 4 ounces to 14 pounds.
2. Make a wood-working lathe and produce an article with it.
3. Invent some means of measuring time which does not require a clock or watch and does not need the sun or other planetary object.
4. Make a rain gauge and a gadget for measuring the velocity of the wind.
5. Make three different types of mousetrap, one of which should be exclusively for white mice.

3

INDOOR PIONEERING

THERE is an interim stage between model and full-scale pioneering and I call this Indoor Pioneering although, in fact, it can be done out-of-doors and quite usefully so done.

The basic thing you need is plenty of Scout staves, for they will be the spars and they will set the size to which you will work.

Now why indoor pioneering? I am going to reel off a few reasons why I used to use it with my Troop.

The first reason is that we could do it at any time of the year whatever the weather. No, we were not afraid to go out, but trying to build a bridge on a foggy evening in February is all right when you are expert but not much good to interest Tommy who came up from the Cubs last week. If we only do pioneering when the weather is perfect then in some countries I know, without mentioning any names, there will not be very much done. My first reason, therefore, is that we can do it at any time of the year whatever the weather and whatever the hours of daylight may be.

The second reason is that even the newest recruit can learn to handle spars of Scout-stave thickness and can learn to lash them, getting a lot of fun and a lot of experience. Some of the projects built full scale are inevitably fairly heavy and not the kind of thing which small boys can tackle with either pleasure or profit.

Reason three is that we can show off a bit, and I think we ought to do so. Pioneering is a very attractive display item for the public but it is not easy to get the public out on a Saturday afternoon to watch us do it. As a display item it takes rather a long time even for our Summer Fête, but Scout-stave pioneering can be done quickly, it can be done indoors during a Parents'

Evening or whatever the occasion (D.C.'s might remember that it has more attraction at an Annual General Meeting than some speakers I have had to listen to), and it does show the parents and the public Scouts in action doing something interesting, exciting, and something which they obviously enjoy. Mind you, it brings a lot of problems in its train.

You will not be able to stick pickets into the Town Hall floor and you will not be able to take up a few planks so that you can get the posts of the sheer legs firmly fixed. You will need to add a lot of extra struts and ledgers and you will need a well-trained Patrol standing by ready for any emergency. I can remember seeing a trestle bridge literally walk out of the door ; it was a very slippery floor ; the trestles were beautifully made and joined together and the idea was that as the bridge was built over a marked stream in the hall the Scouts should run over the bridge. They did this and as they ran the bridge slid along with them, so that the Patrol Leader found his nose against a gas-lit panel marked " Exit ". However, it didn't matter, the bridge stood up all right and the Patrol Leader was none the worse for wear. I don't think anyone who saw the exploit will ever forget it.

Not quite so successful, though, was the flag pole which was carefully laid out along the length of the hall, spar lashed to spar with sheer lashings, guys carefully measured and fixed, and everything immaculately worked out except that no thought was given to the height of the hall. When we came to erect the flag pole we found that it could only be erected at an angle of about 30 degrees to the ground and it looked rather like the neck of a dinosaur as it waved vaguely about to the detriment of the lighting arrangements, to the delight of the spectators, and to the dismay of the Scoutmaster. I can assure you about this because I was the Scoutmaster ! However, even disasters like this are not without value because only a few weeks ago a fellow who was present on this grim occasion reminded me of it and said it had kept him laughing for over twenty years each time he had thought about it.

B

Then there are many unusual features on the inside of buildings that we never find out-of-doors. Indoors in the shape of a hook in the ceiling, or rafter or beam we have that often-longed-for pioneering aid—the Sky Hook—how often have I needed one ! Well, when indoors especially for display purposes, take full advantage of everything the building has to offer and use these unexpected blessings imaginatively so that your projects can take on original forms and give added delight.

Lastly for the Scouter, remember that any activity that will bring a breath of the outdoors into your indoor meeting is a pearl to cherish and to use.

*　　*　　*　　*　　*

TRY THESE IDEAS

6. Devise and make a gadget for stirring the porridge without having to get out of bed. Assume you are in camp and the fire is set at least 10 yards away from your bed.

7. Devise a moving belt system for feeding a Patrol of Scouts who are, for example, tied to their chairs and unable to move anything but their heads.

8. Imagine you are the villain in a "Blood and Thunder" story. You have caught the famous detective. Devise six simultaneous ways of doing away with him so that on the release of one string six different things will happen to him, any one of which would prove fatal. (I suggest you use a dummy for this and not the Scoutmaster.)

9. Suppose the D.C. was stricken with lumbago and found it very difficult to put on his trousers in the morning. Devise an apparatus whereby he could put on his trousers without having to bend.

4

CARE OF EQUIPMENT

IF we are going to do any extensive pioneering we have to face
a reasonable expenditure on ropes, lashings, spars, blocks, and
all the other items necessary for our sort of pioneering. It has
always rather amazed me that Groups and Districts sometimes
seem reluctant to spend money on pioneering equipment to enable
their Scouts to do some real Scouting and yet will spend quite
large sums of money on nicely printed notepaper and other things
which have never seemed to me to be so essential to real Scouting.
It may be, of course, that some Group Committees have provided
equipment and then found that it was badly used so that it
eventually became a complete write-off. There is nothing so
aggravating to a committee as to find a facility abused.

The purpose of this chapter is two-fold. Firstly to say that
you cannot do pioneering unless someone is prepared either to
provide the equipment or to pay for it. When it is provided it
is up to Scouting—and that ought to mean in a good Troop the
Court of Honour and the Scouters—to look after it. Furthermore,
the initial providers or whoever succeeds them must be prepared
to spend a reasonable amount on adding to the equipment and
replacing such equipment as becomes worn. That is the first
side of the picture, but the second side is the main concern of
this chapter, that is, how are we going to look after the equipment?

Buy the best you can afford. Cheap ropes are dangerous,
rotten spars are a menace, and ill-fitting blocks are useless. It
is better to have one good rope than two inferior ropes.

I asked the artist to show you one or two simple points and
if you look at his drawings you will see that he demonstrates
coiling, hanking, and labelling. Let's deal with the latter first.

In the Quartermaster's Store we ought to have a complete and
up-to-date (and that means today) inventory of all the equipment.
I believe a great deal of waste goes on in Scouting simply through

the lack of any record. It must be someone's job, possibly an A.S.M., to keep the inventory up to date and at least once a year to check everything and note its condition. There are various ways of labelling a rope ; the visible way the artist has shown or with some almost secret mark such as putting a different coloured whipping on to the two ends and the middle of the rope. If you adopt this method, mark the middle as well as the ends because the ends are liable to become worn. A good inventory of pioneering gear will not merely be a list of equipment but will indicate quite clearly where it was purchased, how much it cost, and, of course, when it was purchased. This is important because the way to handle ropes in particular is gradually to reduce their status. For example, a rope starts off as the foot-way on a Monkey Bridge or the main rope of an Aerial Runway and perhaps gives us three years' service on that job. We become a little dubious about it and use it for lower level bridging. The years pass and the rope becomes even more worn and perhaps ends its life as the tow rope on a raft, round a camp kitchen, and last of all, something with which to teach recruits how to splice. The point is that merely because you own a rope it does not necessarily mean that it is going to be there permanently ; if it is used it will wear out and our job is to see that it is worn out at its proper economic rate and is not worn out by being misused, or neglected.

To care for a rope the following points must be considered :

1. Before a new rope is put into use strain it. I am sure you don't need me to tell you how to do that. A new rope will have quite an amount of give in it and it may be quite dangerous to use in its new state as, for example, an Aerial Runway, because the amount of give may be so great that half-way down you find yourself unexpectedly making a three-point landing.

2. If we are going to be real pioneers the ropes will get wet quite legitimately from rain or with contact with a pond or river. We must dry them before they are stored, and drying a rope requires space. In the summer, with any luck, you can dry a rope out-of-doors and at Gilwell we lay all ropes in the sun before they are coiled. In the winter the only way is to lay them out in

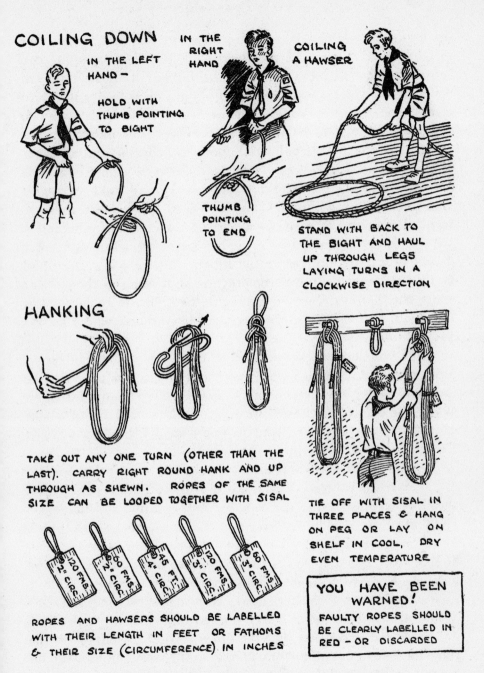

COILING DOWN

IN THE LEFT HAND –

HOLD WITH THUMB POINTING TO BIGHT

IN THE RIGHT HAND

THUMB POINTING TO END

COILING A HAWSER

STAND WITH BACK TO THE BIGHT AND HAUL UP THROUGH LEGS LAYING TURNS IN A CLOCKWISE DIRECTION

HANKING

TAKE OUT ANY ONE TURN (OTHER THAN THE LAST). CARRY RIGHT ROUND HANK AND UP THROUGH AS SHEWN. ROPES OF THE SAME SIZE CAN BE LOOPED TOGETHER WITH SISAL

TIE OFF WITH SISAL IN THREE PLACES & HANG ON PEG OR LAY ON SHELF IN COOL, DRY EVEN TEMPERATURE

120 FMS 2" CIRC.

60 FMS 2" CIRC.

45 FMS 4" CIRC.

120 FMS 3" CIRC.

60 FMS 3" CIRC.

ROPES AND HAWSERS SHOULD BE LABELLED WITH THEIR LENGTH IN FEET OR FATHOMS & THEIR SIZE (CIRCUMFERENCE) IN INCHES

YOU HAVE BEEN WARNED!
FAULTY ROPES SHOULD BE CLEARLY LABELLED IN RED – OR DISCARDED

Methods of Coiling Down, Hanking and Labelling.

the Troop Room, let them drain, turn them so that the air gets to all parts, and then be really satisfied that they are quite dry before putting them away. On the face of it, it would seem easier to coil the rope and put it into a gas oven to dry it. This would dry it, but it would also ruin it. The only safe way to dry a wet rope is to let it take its time and dry naturally.

3. It ought to be a point of honour in Scouting and a matter of tradition in a Troop or Patrol to report any defect in a rope as soon as it happens. The rope may break or a strand get caught in a block and whippings and splicings may come undone. Ideally, of course, the repair would be carried out immediately but that is not always possible. The vital thing is that the repair should be carried out before the rope is put back into store and that on the spot we use an emergency knot, such as the stopper knots, the Thumb Knot or the Figure of Eight, to replace a lost whipping, and the Sheepshank or the Dog Shank where a rope has become frayed.

4. If you look at the drawing again you will see a coiled hawser being fixed to a simple wooden peg. I think a reasonable question is, " How deep should be the coils? " and I suggest $3\frac{1}{2}$ to 4 feet. Put another way, the coils should be of a size suitable for the average Scout to carry on his shoulder without the rope dragging on the ground.

You will notice also that the artist tells you to store the rope in a dry, even temperature. This is not the easiest thing to achieve but certainly we must avoid the rope becoming damp and mildewed and that is best done by ensuring that the air can get at it all round.

5. Suppose the ropes have not been used for some months, how are you going to test them before you put them into action again? You cannot tell just by looking because very often a rope deteriorates from the inside outwards and therefore one should always look *into* a heavy rope at one or two places along its length and make sure that the fibres are not breaking. If the ropes have been out of use for a considerable time then they should be put under strain with a block and tackle just as we did originally when the ropes were new.

6. Now a word to Scoutmasters. We have a responsibility always for the welfare of our Scouts. I am all for adventure and, in fact, this whole book is an effort to help you to make your programmes adventurous, but I do not advocate the kind of adventure that befalls Scouts because the Scoutmaster puts inefficient equipment into their hands. We should certainly teach Scouts how to care for and examine a rope, but in the last resort the responsibility is ours. If a rope breaks it is our fault, and unless we can accept that sort of responsibility and act by it we are not really fit to be Scouters.

Well, I think that is about all I have to say about the care of ropes, except that I should add something about the new materials such as nylon ropes and all the various preservatives that science has discovered, some of which are very good indeed. This is not meant to be a technical book and I am not going to attempt to go into details but I do want to say that I find rope makers extremely helpful and co-operative and their advice is generally to be relied upon. They will always have up-to-date knowledge concerning new types of rope and how various treatments are working out in practice. They will give you more information than any book can hope to do as nowadays things change pretty quickly.

Spars and Pickets : How to Store. Preferably on the ground and preferably flat, supported at intervals of not more than four feet. We have built a very successful Pioneering Rack at Gilwell. The average Troop will not need a big place as it will not attempt to do much pioneering at one time. The structure is made of metal but could be made of wood, and it has a corrugated asbestos roof with no sides or ends because we want the air and to some extent the weather to get at the spars.

The spars are all neatly stacked and easily accessible and that, in itself, means that there is very little damage done when they are brought into action.

Each of the different lengths of spar is marked with a different colour. Therefore, a spar at Gilwell with two red ends we know is twelve feet long; if it has two green ends it is ten feet long, and green and yellow shows that it is eight feet long. Incidentally, we find it convenient to keep our spars in multiples of two feet and we never find any use for spars of five, seven, nine, or eleven feet in length.

What the spars are to be made of is a fairly important point. We need to combine three qualities :

1. Sufficient strength for the job.
2. The minimum of weight commensurate with the strength.
3. The lasting quality of the wood.

On the whole we find Spruce and Larch to be the best woods and these trees have the additional merit of growing straight. It is often possible to get a load from the Forestry Commission when thinning is being carried out. Woods we would not include if we could possibly help it are Willow, Ash—because it is liable to split, Oak—because it is very heavy and rarely grows sufficiently straight for our purpose, but we have done some quite good pioneering with Sweet Chestnut and even with Horse Chestnut. On the whole, however, Larch and Spruce serve us very well.

If you get new larch poles you will find that they are pretty heavy to start with, especially if they are freshly cut, and the first thing we have to do is to strip them of bark. If you leave the bark on, the spar will deteriorate very much more quickly as a sort of mildew forms between the bark and the wood and the spars are also liable to attack by insects. To take off all the bark is quite a task but it is essential. Spars can be creosoted but we do not think it makes very much difference to the life of the wood provided it is stored in the way we advocate. It makes any bridge we build smell very healthy, but you are probably no more concerned with that than I am.

One thing I can only advise you about in general terms is the length and weight of the spars. Obviously, we can build any pioneering project to any size we like, but you know the age of the majority of Scouts in your Troop and it is useless to have equipment that is beyond their physical capacity to handle. The test is never what can the Scouters, the Rover, and the Senior

Scouts handle but what can the twelve-year-old handle. I hope that you will make adequate provision for all ages and I do put in a plea for making pioneering available to the younger boys instead of reserving it as a sort of passing out activity.

As regards the *pickets*; if you do a lot of pioneering you will use a great many pickets. Basically the picket is the end of a broken spar. I have never bought a picket for Gilwell as it is one of the things we produce for ourselves. Take the two ends of a broken spar and put points on the ends. This can be done with an axe but the best way is to do it by the use of fire, scraping off the charred wood. If the job has been well done you will have hardened as well as created the point. The opposite end of the picket must be strengthened by some sort of metal or wire whipping. Whipping with wire, incidentally, is a fairly annoying pastime but it really is essential as the picket is going to be hit frequently with a maul and would otherwise have a very short life.

Well, that deals with ropes, spars, and pickets, and they, after all, are most of it. Buy the best blocks you can afford, look after them; grease the parts that are meant to move and repair immediately the parts which move and are not supposed to do so. Have as good a variety as you can manage; Snatch Blocks, blocks with swivel hooks, blocks with eyes. They all add variety to the pioneering we can do.

Finally, through the care of equipment we can make the Ninth Scout Law a real influence in the life of the Troop. Perhaps if we, as Scouters, set a better example the Scouts would be more ready to follow.

5

OIL DRUM RAFT—MARK I

GEAR REQUIRED

Spars:
Four 15-foot.
One 10-foot.
Four 7-foot.
Three 5-foot.

Lashings:
Two 20-foot.
Thirty-five 15-foot
Cod-line or sisal for oil drums.

Oddments:
The equivalent of ten or twelve
5-gallon oil drums.
Canvas for sail.

I CAN remember as though it were yesterday the first raft I built. I was seven years old and it was my first summer term at school and my very first half-holiday. In the grounds of the school there was a pond. I suppose it was not very large, but at the time it seemed to me to be the biggest lake in the world. In the middle of the pond was an island, thickly grown with bushes and stunted trees, rather dark and forbidding, and yet, to a small boy, tremendously inviting. Well, it was a holiday and I was not supposed to be at school at all but I had found a pal and we managed to get into the school grounds without being caught. We made our way to the lake which was secluded and where we were not likely to be discovered.

All we had with us was a great deal of not very good string but we felt that would be enough. We did not know any knots, had never heard of a square lashing but did know about Robinson Crusoe and, so far as we were concerned, he was a pretty good fellow and obviously until one had built a raft one had not lived. So, we built a raft.

We pulled posts out of the hedge, collected a couple of ladders, found some old oil drums (we might just as well have had sieves for all the use they were), pulled up a plank bridge which went over a ditch leading to the pond, and then, in about ten minutes, we had tied the whole lot together with a sort of cat's-cradle effect. We lugged the finished article to the pond, and what a muddy business it was but you don't mind about mud when you are seven years of age, personally I do not mind much about it now. We pushed the raft into the water and it floated, it floated well until we got on to it, and then it was a very different story. It floated long enough for us to get about five yards from the bank and then, slowly and unspectacularly, it sank, and so did we ! Wet shirts and wet shorts were nothing compared to the disappointment of not reaching the island.

It is true that we could have climbed from the raft and walked to the island but, in the strange way in which boys work things out, that would not have been playing the game and I don't think it occurred to either of us to do it. We got back to the shore, still excited but very disappointed and thought that perhaps a dry pair of shorts would be an improvement.

It is one thing to creep into a place where you are not supposed to be and a very different thing to creep out when every step squelches and there is a perpetual drip, drip, drip as you move along. Oh yes, we were caught ! I suppose we were juvenile delinquents really, now that I come to think about it. We were trespassing, interfering with other peoples' property, and generally being a nuisance, but the master who caught us dealt with us. We were not handed over to a Probation Officer but merely felt the weight of a very heavy hand on a small boy's most receptive part.

So far as one small boy is concerned there were no regrets whatever. That was my first experience with a raft and on the whole the many others I have built and helped to build through the years have never given quite so much pleasure and some have not been very much more successful. However, experience is not to be discounted.

I can help you to build the raft the artist has drawn and to make sure it floats, but I would like you to try one of your own for perhaps it will sink and give you as much fun as my first raft has given me.

Well, to get back to business ; you have seen the list of gear at the beginning of this chapter. It is not very much, just a few spars, a lot of lashings, oil drums, and an old piece of canvas for a sail. I think I can do worse than say a word or two about oil drums. I greatly favour the 5-gallon size ; they are a reasonable proposition to handle and are obtainable, which is an advantage and, on the whole, they do the job we want them to do.

I am not going to try to give you facts and figures about the buoyancy of oil drums ; I am sure there is a formula and I am equally sure that if I knew it and could offer it to you I would not understand it. Any such information concerning oil drums would be misleading because oil drums in my experience are rather similar to a Patrol of Scouts ; they may start off by looking the same but are liable to behave very differently. However, I can tell you some practical things about them. First, don't trust one which is rusty, if it is so old then let it rest in peace. Secondly, beware of those tricky fellows which have a tap as well as a bung. I do not mean that you cannot use them, but there is no use in bunging up the bung-hole and then finding that there is a tap under water which acts like a dive-cock on a submarine.

If you have any choice in the matter try to get a drum which has corrugations on the outside. It is not for me to advertise one make of oil more than another but there is one firm which puts on its oil drums a corrugated ring about 6 inches from either end and they are, consequently, much easier to lash together or on to a spar. Then there is the question of the bung. I know it looks tidy to put all the bungs where they cannot be seen, either facing inwards or under water, but if you do this then you have more confidence in your ability and in the good behaviour of the drums than I ever had. Personally, I put the bungs facing outwards where I can get at them, and I put them above where I fondly imagine the high-water mark will be. Don't rely on a tin cap, a cork or soft wood bung is the best because it will absorb water and will swell and fit tightly. Even when carving a bung you have to be careful, for if it is too evenly

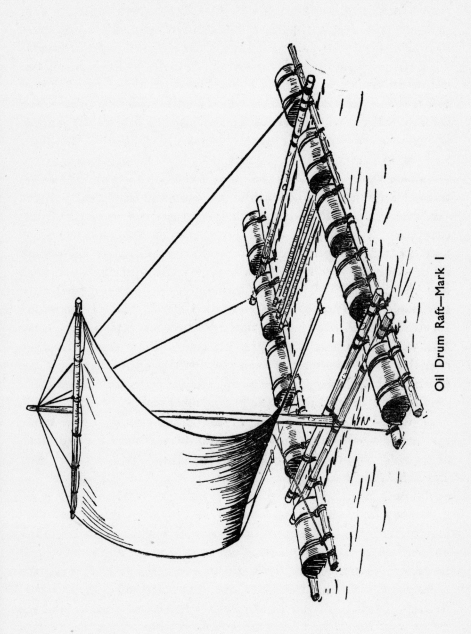

Oil Drum Raft—Mark I

made its very smoothness may defeat you because as it swells it will pop right out. A good bung, strangely enough, is usually a roughly carved one, the sort that can be made without any bother.

If you are going to keep the drums do give them a coat of paint ; it is nice to have them brightly coloured in Scout green, but it is just as effective to use sludge paint which probably any builder will let you have. A good coat of paint on the outside will help to preserve them, and don't forget to paint the ends as well as the sides.

There is, of course, the matter of fixing on the oil drums. So far as I know there is no specific oil drum lashing but I will give you one solid piece of advice, a conclusion reached after bitter experience. Lash each drum quite independently to the frame and don't try to put one long continuous lashing to hold them all in place, for if you do this and one drum works loose you will lose the lot and will sink. However, if you have them lashed separately you can lose one and still have a sporting chance of survival. I see that I have not said anything about buoyancy. You will notice that in the drawing ten 5-gallon drums are used and this particular raft is designed for two fairly hefty people. I believe that four 5-gallon drums will normally hold up a man, so we have four and four and two for luck.

I would like you to look at the drawing. You will make up the two oil-drum ladders independently and fix them a distance apart according to the length of the cross stays you have available. The wider they are apart the more stable the structure will be but it will also be more sluggish in the water.

Then we have the job of fixing the mast ; this is not easy and the artist has missed drawing one or two guys and a fixing for the base. A sort of box affair for the mast to go through is the best, in other words, if you lift up for about a foot two of the cross stays it will help to hold the mast and make it reasonably secure. I think it is very necessary to have the sail fixed in such a way that it can be lowered if the wind changes, otherwise you will just go on and on, so a small pulley block included in the gear will be a help.

There is not very much more to say about the raft, except that I do recommend you to build it fairly near the place where you are going to use it. It is a silly thing with which to walk through the streets and it will be heavier than it appears to be. When you are launching it, do treat it with care ; it is foolish to work hard and produce a good thing and then merely push it off the bank and hope for the best.

Oh yes, you will want a good pole, a Scout stave will do if the water is not more than 4 feet deep, otherwise a quant or long pole will be needed.

Lastly, if any Scouters or Rovers have looked at the picture and said, " We don't want to make a thing like this," maybe the Cubs would like to have a go at it, but don't let Akela know I told you so !

Perhaps the Oil Drum Raft-Mark 2 will test your ability a bit more, so suppose we have a look at it.

* * * * *

TRY THESE IDEAS

10. Devise a towelling machine for a lazy Scout who, after a bathe, cannot be bothered to dry himself.
11. Make a semaphore signalling apparatus which you can operate when concealed at least 10 feet away from any part of the apparatus.
12. Devise and construct a method of signalling morse so that the signals but not the signaller can be seen from the air.
13. Devise a burglar alarm for your Troop H.Q., your Patrol Corner, and your Patrol Camp Site.

6

OIL DRUM RAFT—MARK 2

GEAR REQUIRED

Spars :	Oddments :
Four 15-foot.	The equivalent of ten or twelve
One 10-foot.	5-gallon oil drums.
Four 7-foot.	Canvas for a sail.
Five 5-foot.	One rudder or paddle.
	One heavy plank weighted.
Lashings :	One Handy Billy.
Two 20-foot.	
Forty 15-foot.	
Cod-line or sisal for oil drums.	

WELL, now we are getting somewhere ! This is a much more elaborate affair although most of it is fairly obvious. There are three additions to the Oil Drum Raft-Mark 1, or, more accurately, two additions and one alteration. The alteration is that the two lines of oil drums are slanted to give a bow effect, which will cut the water and enable us to go a little faster. In addition, we have fixed a very crude rudder—I personally think it is a bit too crude—but I am sure you will produce a better one although what I have shown will serve.

We have also introduced—and this is the great feature—a centre-board ; the bit which is shown dark on the drawing is meant to be a lump of old iron or lead (yes, even the " old iron " I said was no use can have its place in Pioneering), although lead is perhaps too valuable to risk. The idea is to have something heavy which will keep the centre board in the water when it is in use. It is fixed, as I hope you can see, on to a spar by two pulley blocks which will allow it to be lowered into the water or to rest above. I am not an expert on sailing and am unable to give you the complete theory about it, but I can

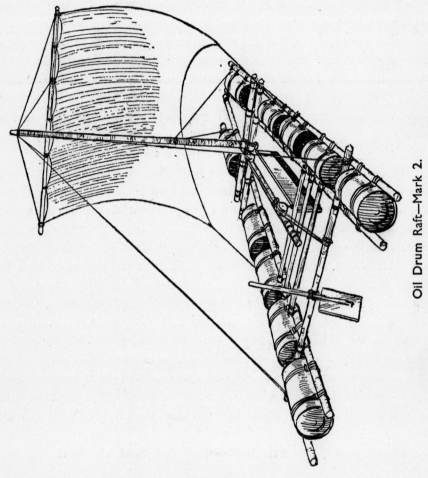

Oil Drum Raft—Mark 2.

tell you that if you have a centre board and you use it with skill you will be able to sail much more accurately on whatever course you choose and you might even be able to sail into the wind as well as with the wind following. You will without doubt, however, find that a craft of this nature needs a lot of room in which to manœuvre.

This being a raft with which one can perhaps go further afield, we might add to the drawing by strengthening the decking. After all, four rather flimsy spars is not a very comfortable platform nor very suitable for a long trip. Planking lashed on would add to our comfort. If the day is hot why not add a canopy? Equally, if the day is wet we would be sheltered from the rain : some of our old tent canvas will fill the need.

There is a delightful story about Baron Munchaussen and thinking of a canopy has reminded me of it. In case you don't know, he was a fabulous German explorer and his stories made Ananias seem like a paragon of truth. One of his stories is that when his horse was unfortunately cut in two as he rode under a portcullis (and incidentally we will offer you a portcullis to make later in the book) he found that half his horse had been left outside and he was only riding on the forepart. He therefore retrieved the other half and stitched the two pieces together with living vines. The vines, being in living flesh, grew and flourished and by draping them over the top he was ever afterwards able to ride sheltered from the rays of the sun and to refresh himself from the fruits of the vine. This is certainly a tall story and it is a pity I do not know of anything which grows in old oil drums.

There is another raft for you in the next chapter.

7

FERRY RAFT

<table>
<tr><td colspan="2">GEAR REQUIRED</td></tr>
<tr>
<td>

Ropes:
  One 2½-inch—longer than width of stream.
  One 1-inch 20-feet longer than width of stream.

Spars:
Eight 6-foot, light.

Lashings:
  Two 15-foot.
  Sixteen light lines.
  Cod-line for oil drums.

</td>
<td>

Blocks:
  One snatch.

Oddments:
  Six or eight 5-gallon oil drums.
  One 6-foot plank for seat.
  Hessian.
  Sisal for mousing.

</td>
</tr>
</table>

THE important thing about this type of raft is that it can be used with safety in a fairly swiftly running stream. Those we have considered in the two previous chapters could not possibly be used where there are rocks or the rate of flow is considerable, and yet this is the kind of stream we might want to cross with a Patrol and perhaps cross quite often if we are camped on one side of it and the village is on the other. This raft is the kind of thing to think about in conjunction with a camp site. Its virtue is that, properly made, it can be used by young Scouts with perfect safety and they will have a great deal of fun and pleasure out of it.

The principle of the raft is simple and, as you see, we have a fixed line between two trees or, alternatively, we could build sheer legs, and the raft is drawn between the two banks of the stream. We are using the sausage method, filling ground sheets with straw, and, of course, the oil drums (incidentally, I have never had the least success with sausage rafts), a pulley on the permanent line and a rope leading from it on to the raft, fixed at two places.

[35]

Ferry Raft.

A point to watch is that you do not, with your permanent line, stop any traffic there may be on the stream and that you do not put the path of the raft over the rockiest part of the stream. I agree, of course, that it would be more fun this way, but it would not be quite so much use.

I might add that the permanent rope needs to be a good one as there will be a lot of strain on it, and the knots holding the raft to the permanent line need to have what I call " and one for luck".

Finally, you do not need a swiftly running stream in which to try out this raft ; obviously it can be tried out anywhere.

*　　*　　*　　*　　*

TRY THESE IDEAS

14. Construct a rope-making machine and also a machine for testing the breaking points of various knots.
15. Make a cuckoo clock.
16. Build a Roman-type chariot.
17. Make a Roman Ballista. (If you don't know what this is, look it up.)
18. Make a scarecrow with enough moving parts to make it seem realistic and capable of being operated from a considerable distance.

8

CORACLES AND OIL DRUM RAFT

ERE are three different types of water-borne pioneering. The first is the *Coracle made from green wood* and covered with light canvas. This is a one-man effort. I do not pretend that it is easy to make, and it is not a thing to hurry. Note that the framework is laid out on the ground. Experience has shown that this is the best way of doing it. If you try

Lay sticks out on the ground.

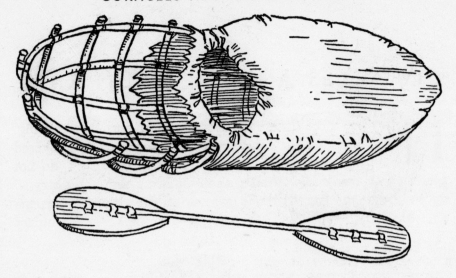

Coracle made from green wood.

to do it in a workshop you get so many slaps across the face from jumping sticks that you will probably give up in despair.

Second is the *Coracle built from sticks and a groundsheet*. (Illustrated on page 40.) You will find it necessary to use a large groundsheet, the tent type rather than a personal one. Buoyancy is given to the coracle by tightly packed brushwood.

Again, we suggest you make the brushwood circle on the ground and the picket method illustrated is very satisfactory. When fixing the groundsheet make sure that the eyelets come on the inside and that the Scout using the coracle is barefoot.

Finally, and most elaborate, is another *Oil Drum Raft*. (Illustrated on page 41.) What I like about this raft in particular is the effort made to raise the deck well above the water-line.

There is a lot of work in this structure, enough to keep the whole Patrol busy for a morning. You could, of course, add a rudder and it would be sensible to have a paddle or a quant to keep you out of trouble.

All you need now, therefore, is " a nice day for a sail ".

TWO CONCENTRIC CIRCLES OF
PICKETS ARE LIGHTLY DRIVEN
INTO THE GROUND & BRUSHWOOD
IS PACKED BETWEEN & BOUND
WITH SISAL. THE HOOP THUS
FORMED IS REMOVED FROM THE
PICKETS, PLACED ON A LARGE
GROUNDSHEET OR TARPAULIN
& SECURELY LACED IN POSITION

Coracle built from sticks and a groundsheet.

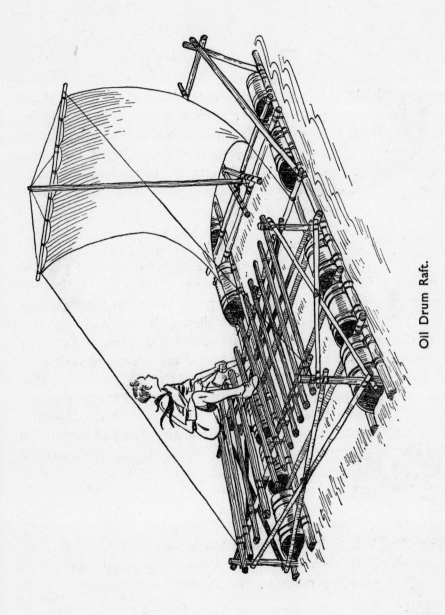

Oil Drum Raft.

9
GETTING WET

No doubt my cynical friends would say that " Getting Wet " could well be the chapter heading of most of the pioneering projects I have encouraged you to try out over the years. I suppose it is true to say that, generally speaking, I have been responsible for more Scouts and certainly more Scouters falling from some sort of apparatus into water than anybody else in the history of the Movement, but I am not making an apology. I have said before that I do not believe anyone is a real Scout until they have fallen in or, more accurately, fallen off. However, most of the things I have talked you into doing have not been planned with the primary intention of making you get wet ; getting wet was merely an incidental pleasure put in for good measure.

This particular chapter I have called " Getting Wet " because with the five things I want to talk about your chances, certainly in the initial stages, of ending dry shod are extremely remote.

Item 1. I call " *The Water Whifflepoof* ". You will recall that the whifflepoof is a log studded with spikes which can be dragged behind a Scout in order to set a trail. The " Water Whifflepoof " is not in any sense concerned with tracking but just provides a pleasant opportunity for a couple of Scouts to test their prowess one against the other. There is little to add to the artist's drawing, except perhaps this : The log should be well-seasoned and should start off comparatively dry and not water sodden ; in short, it should float. The grips must be securely fitted and for once we have abandoned all pretence at lashing and drilled good deep holes, four to six inches deep, and fitted the spars into the drilled holes ; it may be necessary to use wedges to make them fit tightly.

The general idea is that two Scouts mount as shown in the drawing and try, by sheer hard work, agility, low cunning, and the hurling of personal insults, to throw each other off. All we

"The Water Whifflepoof."

really need now is a few fine days in order to enjoy the apparatus to the full.

Item 2.—*Log Rolling*. I expect some of you have seen on films and possibly in real life the Canadian lumberjacks showing off their quite incredible skill in riding rafts and balancing on floating logs. I have been lucky enough to see them in Canada and have been fascinated by them. What has always puzzled me is how they learn in the first place. I have the same kind of bewilderment when I see trapeze artists in the circus. I can see that they do it and do it well and that, so far as they are concerned, there is no real danger. On enquiry I find that nearly all these experts have begun with some adapted apparatus which embodies all the principles of the ultimate object but is so designed that the learner has a sporting chance. We have therefore worked out for all the log-rolling aspirants a simple gadget on which to practise, and the artist has drawn it for you.

Log Rolling.

There are three stages in the process. You will notice the guide line above the log. In the early stages I expect you will spend more time clinging to this line than you will spend on the log. The second stage is to take the line away and the third stage to take all the apparatus away and just leave the log. I wonder how many Scouts will arrive at this stage.

Now to the apparatus itself. We must have good anchorages and we must have blocks with swivel hooks, otherwise the log will merely be fixed firmly in position and will not turn, which would undoubtedly make the whole activity simple but it would be quite pointless. We have shown a block and tackle in action so that the ease of rolling can be adjusted to the weight of the chap using the log. This is not essential but it will make it very much better.

[44]

The Crazy Barrel.

Overhead Line and Barrel
for Crossing Stream.

I do hope you will try this ; it would be grand to see a Patrol of Scouts hiking down the Thames or the Severn, or even the Yarra, with no other means of transport than a log each. Perhaps the day will come !

Item 3.—*The Crazy Barrel*. Gear required : a water-tight barrel, a spar, and a few short lengths of spar to make steps. What the artist cannot show is that there must be some sort of ballast in the bottom of the barrel in order to give it a sporting chance of keeping upright. There is no important pioneering principle involved, but it will train a boy in agility and it may help non-swimmers to become accustomed to the water. My concern in this case is to offer you an hour of activity and good fun during a pleasant day in camp. The spar should go right down to the bottom of the barrel, otherwise it will snap. Experience will show you how tall a spar you can manage, how many rungs you can fix to it, and how high you can climb.

We have only shown one barrel in action but with two barrels

[45]

The Underwater Sea-Saw.

and a couple of those good old-fashioned floor mops there should be a fine opportunity for water jousting.

Item 4.—*Overhead Line and Barrel.*—This is just another way of getting across a stream and not for a moment do I pretend that it is the best or the easiest way. All we need is an overhead line fitted between two trees or two sets of sheer legs, a running block, a rope, a spear, and a barrel. In theory it is possible to have just the barrel but in practice I do not think many of us would get very far. The combination of the overhead line and the barrel really does work, as a great many Scouters on Training Courses at Gilwell have discovered to their amazement and joy.

You might note that the artist has been rather naughty for once and has left out the hook mousing. Knowing him as I do

I think it may be a deliberate omission but, as a friendly adviser, I am warning you !

Item 5. The *Underwater Sea-Saw* involves a little more construction. Two pairs of sheer legs and a log with a plank lashed across the log. There is nothing difficult about it and you will find that the biggest problem is to get the sheer legs to stand in the water : I find that they always float. You may have to tie stones or some other weight to the base of the legs in order to keep them in position, but obviously this will depend upon the bed of the stream or pond. If there is a sandy bottom you can sink the sheer legs a little but you cannot do that if it is a concrete swimming bath you are using. It is rather obvious to remind you that for complete success the two participants need to be of reasonably similar weight. If you forget this you may find you have drowned all your older Scouts. I know there are some in favour of that but I cannot advocate it as a general policy.

Note that the plank is lashed firmly to the light log ; it is the log that moves and not the plank. You can try it the other way if you like, but don't have both swivelling.

I know a number of Scouts are interested in under-water swimming and fishing and this might be another use for those aquatic masks, to say nothing of the miniature " snorkels " I saw a Wolf Cub in Tasmania using with success.

Well, there they are : five interesting projects which I am sure will appeal to any boy who really wants to be a Scout. Put another way, if this sort of thing doesn't appeal to him I wonder what he is doing in the Movement ?

10

TRANSPORTER LADDER BRIDGE

GEAR REQUIRED

Spars :
Two 20-foot.
Two 15-foot or 20-foot.
Two 10-foot.
One 7-foot.
One 5-foot.
Fifteen or twenty 3-foot.

Lashings :
Four 20-foot.
Thirteen 15-foot.
Thirty or forty light lines.

Pickets :
Four.

WHERE you have a stream in a gully or shallow ravine this particular bridge is very useful, as also where the width to be crossed is too wide for an ordinary ladder-type bridge because it would lack support in the centre and probably collapse or else sag too much. This type of bridge can be started on one side of the river and, with any luck, finished on the opposite bank. It embodies two quite simple principles, which we have dealt with several times already, the use of the Scout transporter in a slightly different form, and the use of a ladder made up from spars and short lengths for rungs.

Now the snags : The bottom of the stream needs investigation. As always, when any part of a bridge goes into the water we must have a shot at finding out what is under the water, and this probably means sending a Scout down to test and to find out with a length of pole just what is there. The easiest way of testing is to use a hollow tube, an old piece of gas pipe or a length of bamboo, which you can drive into the bed of the stream for a foot or two to find out the exact consistency of the bed of the stream. In any case, do make sure you know what you are going into and to what extent it will hold up your structure.

Transporter Ladder Bridge.

The second problem is, of course, to get the bearing rail of the transporter at the right height, that is, the rail which supports the ladder. If you get it too high you are going to have an uphill bridge rather like the Tower Bridge when lifted, and if you get it too low then obviously it will not support the ladder and in either case will need a skilled acrobat to use it. There is, of course, a certain amount of adjustment possible after you have set the sheer legs into the water, because the exact angle at which you set the transporter does not matter. Yes, I know that technically it does make a difference but we agreed a long time ago that we were not going to go into higher mathematics about this sort of thing.

The transporter should be built on the bank and I would just remind you that the butts, i.e. the heavy parts, need to go into the water and that your clove hitches on the square lashings must be placed so that they withstand the maximum strain, that is, on the transom of the transporter the clove hitches will be underneath because the ladder will press down on them, and on the ledger they will be on top because the bed of the stream may press up against them.

If the bed of the stream is very soft put on more than one ledger, for example, one which will go under water and one above, and if the stream is any depth you will have to weight the bottom of the transporter otherwise it will tend to float. There is a floating type of bridge in this book but this is not it! The ladder can be constructed in two parts which overlap on the transporter. This will depend upon the material available and on the width of the stream, which is the sort of thing you can decide on the spot. Notice that as always the rungs of the ladder are uppermost, so that when we walk on the bridge we have both a rung and a lashing to support us and do not rely merely on the lashing.

We could add to this bridge by having handrails, but I think it is more interesting to use it without handrails, and it is certainly quicker to build it this way.

I would add to what is shown in the drawing by driving in

pickets at the four ends of the ladder or putting a hefty lump of rock there so that it could not slip in either direction. This kind of precaution one learns by experience.

This is the kind of bridge a Patrol ought to be able to complete in one hour, although it could probably be done in less time if necessary, but in the kind of situation in which you will be building it, it is not advisable to rush as it does need to be solid with the lashings secure.

Lastly, I do not think I would try to bridge a stream more than 15 to 20 feet wide; for wider streams of similar type the next chapter will show you a simple expansion of the bridge we have been dealing with here.

*   *   *   *   *

TRY THESE IDEAS

19. Make an apparatus for blowing up a fire, capable of being worked from at least 10 feet away.
20. Make the following to be worked by remote control :
      A pot lid lifter
      A candle dowser.
21. Make an apparatus for putting wood on the fire without having to go anywhere near the fire.
22. Make from wood and sisal a telescopic flag mast.
23. Experiment with one-man rafts capable of carrying you and your kit.

II

THE DOUBLE TRANSPORTER
LADDER BRIDGE

GEAR REQUIRED

Spars :
Two 20-foot.
Six 15-foot.
Four 10-foot.
Two 6-foot.
Four 4-foot.
Thirty or forty 3-foot.

Lashings :
Twelve 20-foot.
Thirty 15-foot.
Sixty or eighty light lines.

Pickets :
Four.

HERE, as promised in the last chapter, is a bridge suitable for a wider stream. It is a duplication of the Single Transporter Ladder Bridge working from both sides of the stream ; I do not see how you could build this bridge working from one side of the stream only.

Notice that the artist has left out all the guy ropes and the handrail which, in this instance, I should certainly want. The guy ropes are essential.

Just for a change we have put the transporter butts on the bank instead of in the water, and you can vary the structure according to the actual situation, the slope and depth of the banks.

This bridge, I think, is the ideal type for two Patrols to build together and if they plan it carefully, get the measurements right, and start from opposite sides of the stream they ought to meet in the middle and have a really sound and serviceable bridge which will stand up to any test. Here, again, of course, you will probably build up your ladder in sections according to the length of spar and whether you can get the joints of the ladder over the transoms of the two transporters. I think the obvious thing to do is to make three separate sections and lash them

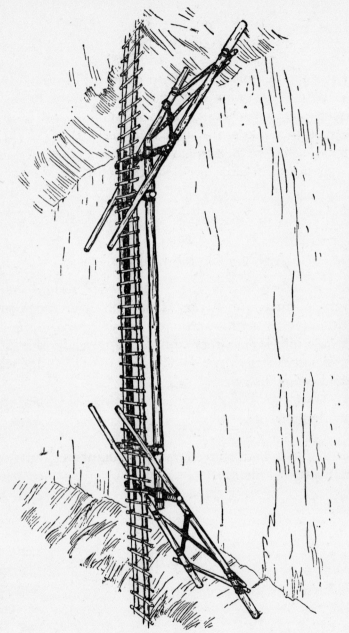

The Double Transporter Ladder Bridge.

together. Notice that the two transporters are both held together and, indeed, held apart by extra spans to the ladder. This is very necessary because this is not the kind of bridge you would want to build in a hurry and there is no use in attempting to bridge a span of 25 or 30 feet without using enough material and making sure the whole thing is substantial and firm.

Finally, if the banks of the stream are rocky then put the butts of the transporter in the stream itself, but if they are muddy then by all means try the method the artist has shown.

*   *   *   *   *

TRY THESE IDEAS

24. Devise a rucksac protector ; some sort of burglar alarm or trap to come into action if anyone opens your rucksac without your permission.
25. Make the following rather unusual camp gadgets :
    (*a*) Clothes drier.
    (*b*) Ironing board.
    (*c*) Iron.
    (*d*) Trouser press.
    (*e*) Coat hanger.
26. Make a loom and with it make a mattress, and use the mattress overnight.

12

PATROL SWING BRIDGE

GEAR REQUIRED

Ropes:
  Four 1-inch, 30-foot.

Lashings:
  One 15-foot.

Spars:
  One 15-foot.
  One 10-foot.

Here is a very simple job, it only needs two spars and four or even three ropes. Mind you, it does not come up to the definition I gave in *Pioneering Projects* about being the sort of thing middle-aged Commissioners would be able to use; this is very much an affair for the Scout with a sense of balance.

The initial problem, of course, is to get the upright pole stuck firmly into the bed of the stream; it does not have to be in very far, but it does have to be in. Well, when building most types of bridge someone has to get wet and it so happens that this is one of that type. How you decide who gets wet is up to the Patrol Leader, with a preference that he should do it himself.

I want to explain the principle of the bridge because it is not very easy to get the idea across by means of a drawing. Loosely attached to the upright is a spar which will reach from the upright to either bank of the stream with a few extra inches to spare. The whole Patrol can start on one side of the stream and whoever is chosen to go across will place the spar in the middle of the four Scouts who are holding the guy ropes. The Scout who is crossing will run out along the spar and grasp the central pole, and he will need to be agile to do it! It is useless to edge along gingerly as this courts disaster; keep your eyes

[55]

Patrol Swing Bridge.

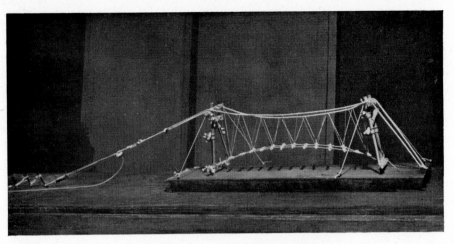

A MODEL OF A SUSPENSION BRIDGE

TARPAULIN RAFT WITH OUTBOARD MOTOR

RAFTS

UNDERSIDE OF
'KON TIKI'
WITH DRUMS
AND INFLATED
BUOYS IN POSITION

ALTERNATIVE METHOD
OF ATTACHING INFLATED
BUOYS

OIL
DRUM
RAFT-
MARK I

RAFTS

'KON TIKI'
SETS
SAIL

PREPARING
SUPPER

'KON TIKI'
AT
ANCHOR

A RAFT
NEGOTIATES A
DERRICK BRIDGE

open and make a dash for it and you will soon grasp the central pole. (If you miss, you're in !) Having done that—using your feet as levers, work the spar away from the bank you have left and swing it round to rest on the far bank. Meanwhile the four Scouts with the guy ropes will have been working both independently and in unison to keep the centre spar upright, or leaning slightly towards the opposite bank. Once again, when the point of the spar is on the bank you will have to dash for it.

Well, let's assume that you are safely over. One of the Scouts will throw his guy line over to you ; it will, of course, still be fixed to the top of the upright spar, and you will swing the horizontal spar back to him. He will then cross as you did, the only difference being that you will be taking some of the strain on the upright spar from the other side of the stream. When all the Scouts are finally over you can, if you like, pull the apparatus in after you.

I know all this sounds complicated, and I expect someone has remarked that it is impossible. Believe me, it is very simple. I have had dozens of Scouters on Course at Gilwell doing this ; I have done it myself, and up to now I have not been in the water. It is grand fun, requires the absolute minimum of gear, and it really does work.

However, if you would like to tackle something a little more elaborate then take a look at the next chapter.

13

REVOLVING DERRICK BRIDGE

GEAR REQUIRED

Ropes :
One 2-inch, 30-foot.
One 2-inch, 15-foot.
One 1-inch, 30-foot.

Spars :
One 15-foot.
Two 10-foot.
Two 3-foot.
Ten 2-foot.

Lashings :
Five 15-foot.
Twenty light lines.

Pickets :
Four.

Blocks :
One single-sheave.

Oddments :
One 2-inch strop–2-foot.

THIS is a more general version of the project in the last chapter. The principle is very similar and very simple ; merely an upright spar bedded in the middle of the stream. (Incidentally, all these things are useful over marshy ground as well as over streams.) For this we use a ladder, either an ordinary one or one made up, and this is obviously very much easier to walk across than the spar we used in the last chapter, and we have introduced a pulley. I think the drawing makes quite clear the function of the pulley. The introduction of a longer guy rope means that instead of the fellow who has walked over the bridge doing the swinging round of the ladder one of his fellows on the bank does the pulling.

Now to describe the operation. The actual construction is obvious from the picture, but its use is not quite so obvious. The Scout who is going to cross walks over the ladder to the central pole ; he will hold on to the central pole and will give a signal—it is a good thing to have this clear otherwise the operators are liable to go into action too quickly—and the Scout

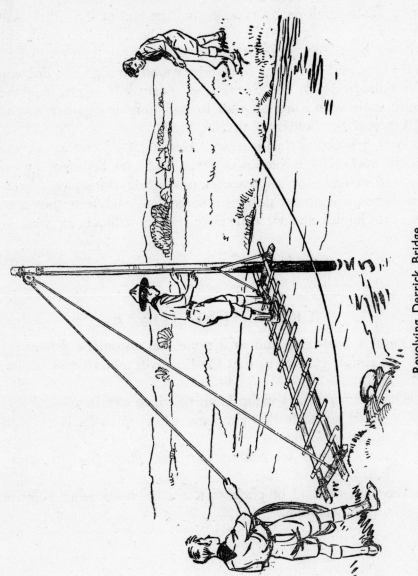

Revolving Derrick Bridge.

on the left bank who has the pulley part under control will gently, repeat gently, pull on his rope so that the end of the ladder will lift away from the bank ; whereupon the other Scout on the opposite bank (no comment as to how he got there) will pull on his rope and will swing the ladder round through 180 degrees. It remains only for the Scout who meanwhile is grasping the central pole with some anguish to pull himself together and to walk across the ladder to the far bank.

Well, I hope all that is clear. Here again, I can assure you that it works. It is simple to make and uses little equipment but it does embrace some useful pioneering principles. However, if you still do not think it is sufficiently elaborate then read the next chapter and we will make it more difficult for you.

*   *   *   *   *

TRY THESE IDEAS

27. Build a bird-table and to it attach an automatic release for a simple camera so that the bird will take its own photograph.

28. Devise a gate for a camp kitchen, which can be opened and closed satisfactorily by a Scout whose arms are laden with dishes of food.

29. Make a gadget for raising your hat when your arms are laden.

30. Devise a method of pitching a tent without using poles of any description.

14

DERRICK DRAWBRIDGE

GEAR REQUIRED

Ropes:
Two 2-inch, 10-foot.
Two 1-inch, 20-foot.

Spars:
One 15-foot.
Four 10-foot.
Twenty 2-foot.

Lashings:
One 20-foot.
Forty light lines.

Blocks:
Two single-sheave.

Now, you see, we have advanced to two ladders; the whole thing is becoming more elaborate and more extensive. This erection, like the drawbridge of old, will enable you to seclude your camp site, if it is that kind of place, so that no unheralded person can enter. Either side of the bridge can be drawn up and secured by taking a couple of turns round the central pole, and just as quickly it can be put into operation.

The difficult part of this bridge, and the previous two with which we have dealt, is to get that centre pole fixed into the ground. The best advice I can give you is to take an old picket into the centre of the stream and make a hole with the picket quickly slipping the butt of the main spar into the hole the picket has made. If the bed of the stream is firm it is quite easily done, but if it is sandy or silted then you will probably have to drive in pickets to surround the upright spar and possibly pile boulders around as well.

In these three chapters I have intentionally offered you something rather more simple than we have been dealing with up to now. I do not think we want to go on getting more and more complicated and I am anxious to offer you as much pioneering experience as possible using as little gear as I possibly can.

Derrick Drawbridge.

15

TASSIE

GEAR REQUIRED

LIFTING SECTION ONLY:

Ropes:

One 2-inch, 30-foot.
One 2-inch, 20-foot.

Spars:

Seven 15-foot.
Three 10-foot.
Four 5-foot.
Ten or fifteen 3-foot.

Lashings:

Two 20-foot.
Eighteen 15-foot.
Twenty or thirty light lines.

Blocks:

One single-sheave.
One double-sheave.

EACH SECTION OF THE PONTOON:

Spars:

Two 10-foot.
Eight or ten 3-foot.

Lashings:

Two 15 foot.
Twenty-eight or thirty
light lines.

Oddments:

Two pickets.
Six 5-gallon oil drums.

I CAN almost hear you saying " What on earth does he mean ; why give a queer-looking affair like this an even odder name ? " I hope all my friends in Australia will still be my friends after they have read on but, as a matter of fact, I got the idea for this bridge when I was in Tasmania and drove across the quite wonderful bridge which spans Hobart Harbour.

Most of us in other countries are apt to forget Tasmania, but I have a great affection for the place ; it is really lovely and the people I met there are charming. Hobart Harbour I consider is one of the natural wonders of the world. I can say this because, whilst I have not seen all the great harbours of the world I have seen a good many. They forget to teach you quite a lot at school because, whilst I knew all about Sydney Harbour, the Golden Gates of California, and numerous others, I did not

[63]

even know there was a harbour at Hobart. It is strictly true that it is big enough to take at one time all the shipping in the world. It is a very deep harbour and I think I am right in saying that it is 40 feet deep right at the quayside, although I suppose I should have said nearly seven fathoms.

The bridge across the harbour is, as far as I know, of a unique type ; it is shaped in an arc, the point of the arc being seaward, and the majority of the bridge, about three-quarters of it, is a pontoon type of structure although it has a perfectly sound roadway across it. At the end, nearest to the quay of Hobart, there is a lifting section, complete with roadway, and this can be raised to allow great ships to pass through.

The first bridge of this type which they built was swept away in a terrible storm and the present one which has been there for some years is protected by a breakwater. I gather from my Tasmanian friends, however, that bets are freely offered and taken as to the fate of the bridge whenever the weather is rough.

I do not pretend for a moment that the drawing in this chapter will be in any way familiar to any resident of Tasmania and I only repeat that when I first saw Hobart Harbour Bridge I was very impressed with it and hoped it would give me an idea for a Scout bridge. Well, this is it !

Now what about building it ? Oil-drum pontoons with a ladder across which could be planked over to make a better roadway ; this does not require any explanation. If you cannot by this time lash an oil drum on to a spar with a sporting chance of it staying there then start again and get to grips with Chapter I of *Pioneering Projects*. I might just point out, however, that if the river on which you are building this bridge is tidal, then at the fixed end you will need to make your fixing lines loose in the sense that they will allow the oil drums to rise and fall with the changing level of the water. There is nothing difficult about doing this, but it is foolish to have a bridge which is meant to make contact with the water and doesn't do so, and it is sillier still to have a bridge which, instead of being level, lies at an angle of 45 degrees.

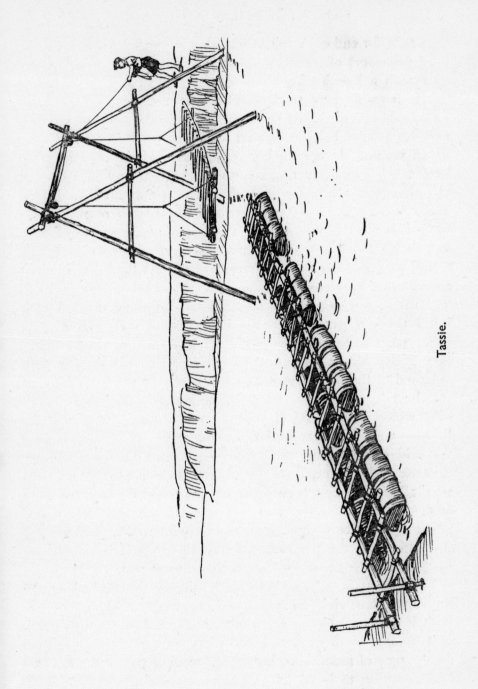

Tassie.

At the far end of the oil drums, that is, in midstream, you will need some sort of sea anchor but this need be no more than a rope with a bunch of old iron on the end of it.

(It is rather strange that in an earlier chapter of this book I said that you could use in pioneering everything except old iron and yet I have twice suggested a use for it.)

In making the sea anchor remember that the rope must be long enough to carry the iron to the bottom and to allow for any change in the water level, otherwise it may hold the bridge under water. Now we come to the lifting part of the bridge but this is not really difficult. The length of the sheer legs, etc., will be governed by the depth of water in which we are going to put them. Note that the crossbars are fixed at such a height as will allow easy passage along the bridge when it is in position. The artist, not being very tall, has not bothered to show this, but I think it would be better if you could make the holding ropes meet very much higher than is shown in the drawing. The pulley blocks are lashed to the crossbar and that, in turn is lashed to the sheer legs. You will probably need guy lines on the sheer legs but these can easily be added.

I would be inclined to put oil drums under the part of the bridge to be lifted, as well as on the pontoon section, as they will take a lot of strain away from the structure when the bridge is in use and will round off the job and make it neat. Of course we shall need a fixing between the pontoon and the lifting sections as you cannot hope for it to go up and down and always land in the right place without leaving a gap. I would suggest using strops fixed to the pontoon end and these could be lifted over the butts of the lifting end when they are at water level.

Well, that is "Tassie" for you. Every time I look at the drawing I have vivid memories of Tasmania, but when you have built it once or twice it will probably remind you not so much of Tasmania or of its duck-billed platypus and mysterious lakes on the tops of mountains, but it will remind you of the fun you had in trying to build it.

16

THE LOOKOUT LIFT

GEAR REQUIRED

Spars :
Six 10-foot.
Thirty 2-foot.

Blocks :
Three sets Handy Billies long enough to
reach from branches to ground.
1–3-sheave for synchronising hauling ropes.

Lashings :
Fifteen 15-foot.
Sixty light lines.

Oddments :
Hessian.
Sisal for mousing.

No doubt as you look at the drawing on page 69 many of you will say " Now what on earth is that ? " and from one point of view I would find it difficult to give you an answer because I would have to admit that there are easier ways of climbing a tree. I cannot conceive of the apparatus being put into large-scale production for the home or export market, but ever since I can remember I have enjoyed doing the things I wanted to do, whether or not there was any particular point in them, and especially have I enjoyed doing things where there is a bit of fun round the corner and a small element of risk. I think there is a lot of fun to be got from playing about with this rather odd structure.

This particular idea came to me when I was looking at a model of an old galleon ; I saw that there was a queer sort of combination lookout and lantern built like a rather large serviette ring to slide up and down the mainmast. The memory of this model stayed with me a long time and suddenly I thought of using the same principle for a lookout post.

Obviously, the first thing to select is the tree. This seems to be a ridiculous sort of remark, but you cannot build round any sort of tree. (Try it on a Monkey Puzzle if you doubt me.) We need one with a reasonably straight bole and where the lower branches are at least 30 feet above the ground. We built this several times at Gilwell round an Ash which seemed to be conveniently designed for our purpose, but there are many other types which might suit ; the Scots Pine comes readily to mind as one likely to fill the need. The trees most likely to be unsuitable are the Oak, which usually has a thick trunk and not enough of it, the Hawthorn, for the very good reason that it pricks where it hurts and rarely grows to a reasonable height, the Elm (although the Wych Elm might be all right), because it is dangerous and liable to shed one of its main branches, and any trees which are unstable as to growth or roots, such as the Willow on the side of a stream.

How are we going to build the affair ? Try as I may, I have not yet found any system of making a success of this without someone having to climb the tree (dropping by parachute on to the tree is liable to be expensive and would take rather a long time, besides being uncertain in its results). As we have ropes it is not difficult to climb the tree, for it is not beyond our skill to cast a weight over one of the branches and pull the rope after it. With the help of the rope it should not be difficult to climb up and find a comfortable position in the tree. The rope, of course, will be useful for hauling up the blocks and the lashings needed to fix the blocks to the branches. This is one of the most important jobs. It is necessary to get them in the correct places, and this means knowing the exact sizes of the platforms, to get them fixed very firmly, and to protect the tree with sacking.

If you are lucky enough to have blocks with hooks attached, a fixed loop of rope round the branch and doubled, the hook slipped through it and the hook moused, i.e. the point of the hook covered over and whipped back to the point, will serve very well and make the matter quite simple, but if you have to be satisfied with blocks without hooks the job is still possible, although not so easy, because all blocks have provision made for a rope or wire fixing. When the blocks are firmly fixed, haul up the ropes and run them through the blocks.

Lookout Lift.

Meanwhile the team on the ground will have been building the platform round the tree. It is important, incidentally, to remember to build it round the tree as it is rather difficult to slip it over the tree after it is made ! I hope you have noticed that the artist has shown the rungs of the ladders on top of the spars.

The main hoist ropes should be fixed with a bowline where the ladders cross at the three points of the triangle, and preferably on the outside edges as shown, although in some situations it may be found better to vary this.

Finally, we come to using the gadget. My friend, the artist, has slipped up a little in two ways. In the first place he ought to have shown some method of tying the hoisting ropes to pickets on the ground so that when the lift is in the air it need not be kept there by people holding the ropes, which is apt to be tiring. Secondly, the artist is in error with the fellow actually on the lift. Looking at the drawing I can almost see the boy getting a wallop on the top of the head. He ought to be looking upwards so that he can avoid bumping into the branches and because it is so much safer, especially if you are unused to heights to look upwards until you are accustomed to being in the air, when you can look round and then down.

Well, there it is then, but don't wait for the summer ; you can see so much more on a clear day in the winter when the leaves are off the trees.

17

RUSTIC TOWER AND DOUBLE LOCK TRESTLE BRIDGE

THE drawing shown overleaf is a working drawing made by Scouts and Scouters who did in fact build the project shown.

Quite deliberately, in the books I have written on pioneering, I have avoided giving any set scheme or anything that in any sense could be taken to be an engineering drawing. I have tried to give you ideas and a little advice born out of experience. I did not want you merely to be copyists but to have the adventure of working things out for yourself. Nonetheless, for any large project it is essential that somebody should try to make a working drawing of the project and this, which as you see, comes from Workington in Cumberland, is a very good example : it is not a highly finished drawing but it is a very adequate, clear, and accurate plan.

From the Scoutmaster's point of view, the degree of enthusiasm in the Troop or in the Patrol will never be uniform ; some boys will not like the hard work of erecting a tower and the heavy lashing entailed, but those boys may well find an outlet for their energy in planning and producing the working drawings. Just as indeed with the Troop Show, some like to star in front of the footlights whilst others take their pleasure and get their training from working the lights, painting the scenery, or selling the programmes. The adventurous will wish to be first on top of the erected tower while some boys will prefer the back room job with pen and ink and paper and a more theoretical approach. Scouting has room for all types and this is another way of appealing to a particular type.

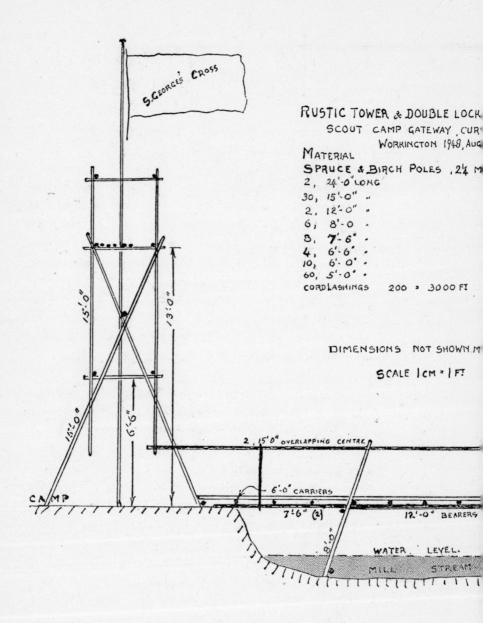

S. GEORGES CROSS

RUSTIC TOWER & DOUBLE LOCK
SCOUT CAMP GATEWAY, CUR'
WORKINGTON 1948, AUG

MATERIAL
SPRUCE & BIRCH POLES . 2½ M
2, 24'-0" LONG
30, 15'-0" "
2, 12'-0" "
6, 8'-0 .
8, 7'-6" .
4, 6'-6' .
10, 6'-0' .
60, 5'-0' .
CORD LASHINGS   200 × 3000 FT

DIMENSIONS NOT SHOWN M

SCALE 1 CM × 1 FT

15'-0"

13'-0"

15'-0"

6'-6"

2, 15'0" OVERLAPPING CENTRE

6'-0" CARRIERS

CAMP

7'-6" (2)

12'-0" BEARERS

8'0"

WATER LEVEL.

MILL   STREAM

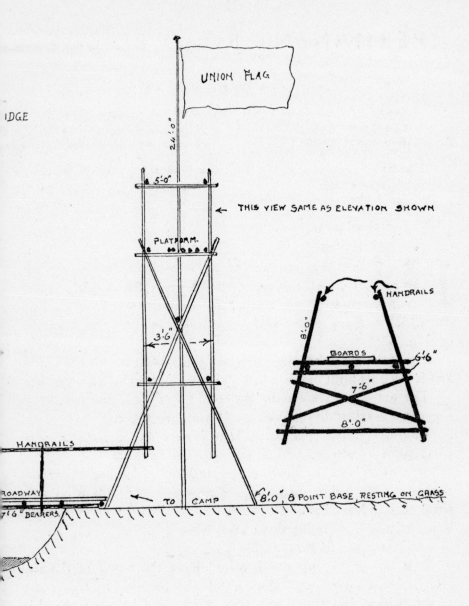

IDGE

UNION FLAG

24'-0"

5'-0"

← THIS VIEW SAME AS ELEVATION SHOWN

PLATFORM

3'-6"

HANDRAILS

8'-0"

BOARDS

6'-6"

7'-6"

8'-0"

HANDRAILS

ROADWAY

← TO CAMP

8'-0", 8 POINT BASE RESTING ON GRASS

7'-6" BEARERS.

18

PERMANENT ROAD BRIDGE

GEAR REQUIRED

Ropes :
   Two 2-inch, 40-foot.
   Two 2-inch, 30-foot.

Spars :
   Thirteen 10-foot.
   Ten 7-foot.
   Fourteen 5-foot.
   Twenty or thirty 3-foot.

Lashings :
   Thirty-two 15-foot.
   Forty or sixty light lines.

Oddments :
   Hessian.

IN this project we are again, as it were, evolving on the transporter, but the suggestion here is for a rather more permanent structure where, for example, you have a camp site which is going to be used a lot and is bounded by a stream or a gully.

This job will take quite a time, probably several weekends, and it must be built in fairly heavy timber and really substantially.

The artist has shown the skeleton framework and I want to suggest several additions you could usefully make.

In the first place, a permanent bridge should have a more permanent roadway, which you can make either by lashing extra rungs cheek by jowl or by lashing planks or half-sewn timbers in the other direction. I do think you will need permanent handrails, and the centre of the bridge gives a good base on which to build them and, indeed, indicates the height at which to put them.

If it was my camp site I would have the name of the site and perhaps a welcome sign carved and hanging at the centre of the bridge, but make sure that it does not hang so low that the " welcome " would make a physical impact on the visitor !

Properly built, this type of bridge would not need any guy ropes although when in process of building it you will need a

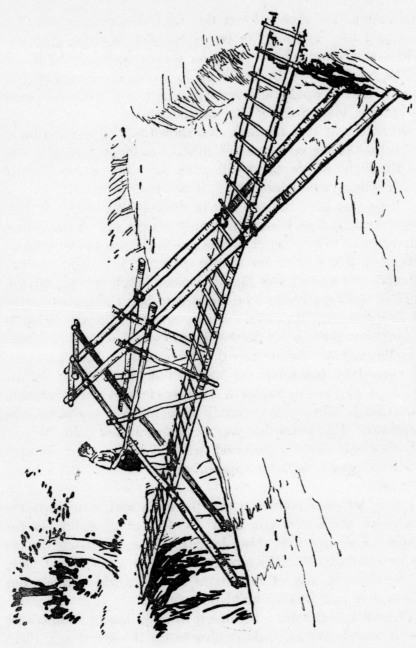

Permanent Road Bridge.

certain amount of rope to lower the two transporter sections into place, and they will need to be guyed back to trees or pickets whilst you are actually working on the bridge.

The roadway can be made up in sections ; I suggest four sections, and I would add bearers where the roadway passes through the long spars of the transporters.

Do take note that the artist has shown a good overlap on to the banks. It is a very common mistake to forget this point and then the slightest movement will make the bridge wave about in mid-air which, whilst interesting, is not very practical.

I hope you have noticed that in dealing with many of these bridges we started with something quite simple and by easy stages we have come to a rather elaborate and fairly permanent bridge ; permanent, that is, if we use decent spars and lash them together properly. As a matter of fact, if I were building a permanent bridge of this type I would be inclined to bolt the spars together and then lash over the bolts. I hope no one is horrorstricken at the idea, but there is no lashing in the world which will stand up to the English climate month after month without loosening and eventually becoming too weak to do its job. If we are building a permanent bridge it is quite right to use permanent aids. Coach bolts would certainly be included in my pioneering equipment. I do stress that you use bolts and not nails, because nails are liable to split the wood, whereas before using the bolt we will, of course, drill the appropriate size of hole with a brace and bit.

Lastly, let me remind you that the main spars can be on the bank or in the water, you must decide that according to the situation, the important thing is that you so design the bridge that the roadway is level—mountaineering is a very good thing but there are plenty of mountains in the world without our going out of our way to build our own !

There is a final point ; because it will take longer and because there is more work in it, do resolve to try it some time ; there really is tremendous satisfaction in undertaking a big job of this nature and carrying it through to a successful conclusion.

19

PYRAMID TOWER

GEAR REQUIRED	
Spars :	**Lashings :**
Three 16-foot.	Five 20-foot.
Three 14-foot.	Fifteen 15-foot.
Three 12-foot.	Twenty-six light line for plat-
Three 6-foot light.	form and ladder.
Twelve staves from 6 feet to	
2 feet.	**Oddments :**
	Rope ladder.

THIS project embodies a pioneering principle which we have not used up to now. The idea was born out of the Festival of Britain Skylon, but I am inclined to think that what I am suggesting here is more use.

You will see quite clearly from the drawing that the structure is composed of two similar three-sided pyramids which are lashed together and held in place by short guy ropes. There is really very little to say about the building of it : I hope it is obvious that the right way to tackle the job is to build two pyramids quite separately, and to build them with the longest sides on the ground, and then join them together as shown and pull them erect, using long guy ropes for the purpose. Incidentally, this job of erection is great fun and calls for good team work. Obviously if you do not attach the ropes in the right place it will not go up, and if you pull too hard it is liable to go right over, which is exciting but not very much use.

There are several small points I would like to mention :

The first is that a Figure of Eight Lashing must be used where the three spars meet on each pyramid. Secondly, as the artist has shown, sink the butts of the base pyramid into the ground for 3 or 4 inches to give it a secure footing. Thirdly, make sure the rope ladder is in place before erecting the structure

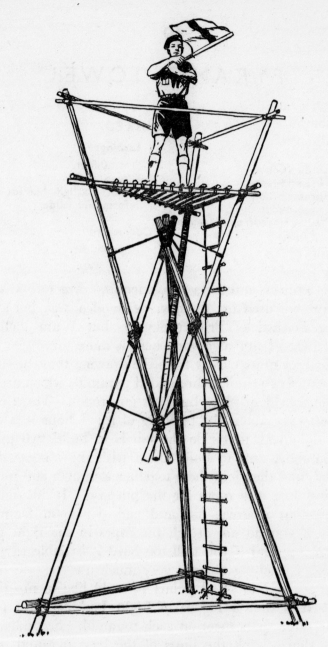

Pyramid Tower.

as it is very awkward to try to put it on afterwards. Fourthly, do not forget to include handrails.

The advantage of this type of structure is that providing you have enough spars it can be made quite quickly and two Patrols ought to be able to erect it in less than an hour. If for any reason you do not want your observation post to be seen from a distance it is very easy to lower it on to its side after use and then it is ready for erection at very short notice.

The project lends itself very well to indoor pioneering; carried out with Scout staves it could be a very effective and a quickly built display item. Two of them in a large hall at, for example, a Parents' Evening, would enable you to provide a worthwhile demonstration of signalling. I might add that signalling is not its only use; it would make an excellent perch for an Air Spotter, is certainly worth considering for nature spotting, and those of you who are keen photographers will get some interesting shots of a camp site from the top of such a structure. Anyway, I hope you will try it; it has been built at Gilwell several times and has always been successful.

*   *   *   *   *

TRY THESE IDEAS

31. Invent a really useless gadget for a really pointless purpose. (This sounds absurd but it produces worthwhile results if the spirit in the Patrol is right. The instructions can be extended to "include one moving part" or "must be portable".)

32. Join two staves together using rope but avoiding any lashing and any knot other than the Figure of Eight. (This idea ought to open a new field of thought to imaginative Scouters. There are all kinds of things we can learn about which are useful and interesting to do.)

[79]

20

STILT TOWER

GEAR REQUIRED

Ropes :
Two 1-inch, 50-foot.

Spars :
Two 20-foot.
Two 12-foot.
Four 6-foot, light.
Four 5-foot, light.
Sixteen 6-foot staves.
Four 3-foot staves.

Lashings :
Nine 15-foot.
Fourteen 10-foot.
Thirty light lines.

Pickets :
Four.

Oddments :
Rope ladder.

THIS is a fairly obvious structure, the main requirements being two long and really stout spars to carry the platform. We should build it on the ground and then pull it into place using guy ropes, and the two main spars should be firmly placed in holes already prepared for them. They need to be 12 to 18 inches in the ground to be really secure.

The lashings on this project need to be 100 per cent, especially in the case of the two square lashings where the platform is fixed to the two upright spars : these two lashings are the crux of the whole structure.

As to the rest of it, you can use quite light materials, Scout staves would do, for handrails and the V-shaped supports. It might be a good idea to use a guy line hitch on bracing guys or just an ordinary tent guy-line runner.

This tower I think could well be built on a permanent camp site, and if you happen to have access to a piece of ground affording a good view it would be very fine to have on the tower a board clearly marked with compass directions and pointing out the places of interest which can be seen from the tower.

Stilt Tower.

Another use for all these towers is to teach Scouts to use maps. Get up there with a map, learn to set it, identify the objects in the distance and then find them on the map ; you can also see the lie of the land, afforestation, the curve of rivers, etc., and the whole map will come to life.

Now I want to suggest taking it a stage further. See if you can design your own signalling platform using just one upright spar ; it is by no means impossible and it is obviously a step forward from the one I have given to you here.

*   *   *   *   *

TRY THESE IDEAS

33. Devise and make a remote control wasp-catcher capable of being operated successfully when the operator is in a sitting position, and capable of giving full coverage for a full circle round the operator.

34. Invent a device for raising a flag to the masthead, to operate automatically as a gate is opened and, likewise, for the flag to be lowered as the gate is shut.

35. Design a similar device so that a flag will run up to the masthead and fly when any notability steps on to one or other of the bridges contained in this book. The flag should rise entirely by the physical contact made by the notable person with some part of the bridge.

36. Design and make a Camp Rouser capable of being operated by the Troop Leader or Patrol Leader whilst he himself is still in bed.

21

LAZY MAN'S GATE-OPENER

GEAR REQUIRED

Ropes :
One 1-inch, 55-foot.

Spars :
Two 5-foot.

Lashings :
One 15-foot.

Blocks :
One single sheave.

Oddments :
Gate.

THERE could not be any simpler pioneering project than this one and yet I think it has a practical use on a camp site or at the entrance to a Scout Headquarters.

This particular design assumes that the gate has a spring which will cause it to shut slowly after you have passed through it and our job is to devise a means of opening the gate against the spring, driving a car through the gate, and letting it shut behind the car.

All you need is a fairly long rope and a block, with a tree or pole to which to fix the block. I have no doubt the contraption contravenes some section or other of the Highway Code but as you will not be putting it into practice on the highway it will not matter.

Don't write to me and say you do not possess a motor-car because it will work equally well from a bicycle or on foot, and when you have done it try to devise a means of working it from the other way as well, but the next project will show you how this can be done.

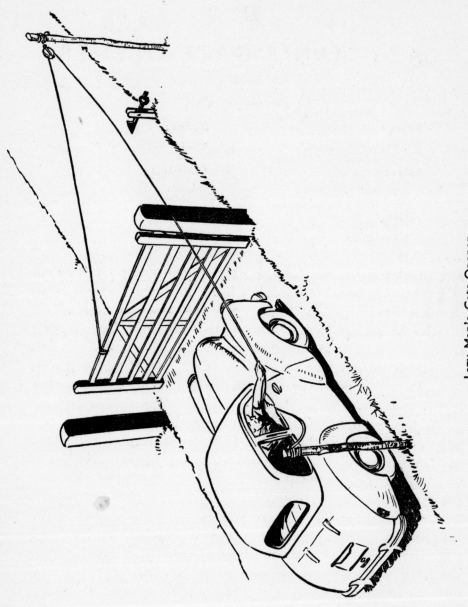

Lazy Man's Gate-Opener.

22

COUNTERPOISE GATE

GEAR REQUIRED

Ropes :
One 1-inch, 35-foot.

Spars :
One 20-foot.
Three 15-foot.
Three 10-foot.
Six 6-foot.
Two 5-foot.
Four 4-foot.
Two 3-foot.

Lashings :
Three 20-foot.
Ten 15-foot.
Eighteen light lines.

Blocks :
Three single-sheaves.

Oddments :
Tree butt for weight.

HERE we have built our own gate and included a trick device for opening it, operated by the passenger in the car.

The drawing on the next page is self-explanatory except that perhaps I ought to explain that the whole affair is supposed to be so well balanced that at whatever point you stop pulling on the rope the gate will remain in that position. It is, of course, tedious to cut lumps from a log until it is exactly the right weight, but if you remember the Counterweight Bridge in *Pioneering Projects* you will recall that in addition to a fixed weight we used a variable weight which was merely a bag of sand or earth. You may find that to incorporate something like that in this case is worthwhile.

I have shown you the simple outline which, incidentally, you can duplicate quite easily so that it can be worked from the opposite side of the gate. I suggest you try this, find out the snags, improve on it, and try to elaborate it. All the time you are playing about with a thing of this sort you are improving your experience and your technique for more important pioneering projects. The chap who can make a comparatively useless automatic gate is the fellow who, when he needs to do so, can build a bridge on which a lot depends.

Counterpoise Gate.

23

COUNTER BALANCE GATES

THE artist shows you two rather pleasant suggestions, a little more ornamental than the gates usually seen in camp but, I think, worth the extra trouble.

There are only two points to make : the first is that you have to learn how to make netting, and this has infinite uses, for fishing, making hammocks or, as here, purely ornamental use. The second and perhaps more vital point is that the counterweight should balance perfectly so that the gate can be opened by the touch of a finger and will hold in place automatically.

Note also the use of the old tin in the second gate to give it ease of movement. You will find that a round stone just slightly let into the base of the upright pole and working on the base of the tin will give an excellent movement.

Again, I cannot in any sense pretend that gadgets of this nature are essential to Scouting, but it is no bad thing in a permanent camp to have an attractive entrance and even for your Summer Camp it is worth taking the trouble to have some sort of pretentious approach and at the very least show a visiting Commissioner that somebody in the Troop can do a little lashing and you have not come to camp merely to laze in the sun and have a holiday.

*   *   *   *   *

TRY THIS IDEA

37. Build a trestle using only two lashings and for the other two corners use a strop. N.B.—No knot is to be tied in the strop.

Counter Balance Gates.

24

PORTCULLIS DRAWBRIDGE

GEAR REQUIRED

Ropes :
One 1-inch, 50-foot.

Spars :
Four 12-foot.
Two 10-foot.
Two 7-foot light.
Fourteen 6-foot light.
Eighteen 6-foot staves.
Two 2-foot.

Lashings :
Four 20-foot.
Fifty-four 10-foot light.

Pickets :
Two.

Blocks :
One double-sheave.
One single-sheave.

Oddments :
Cable reel.

I APPRECIATE very fully that this project is comparatively useless and a lot of nonsense ; in fact it is very hard to find any justification for making it, except that it is amusing, it will undoubtedly add to your experience and, carried out in the right spirit, it is a lot of fun to build. I am sure you will agree with me that this is almost out of the realms of fantasy.

I had better explain what it is all about, although I think the artist has done a more than usually good job in translating into pictures what I told him. What is supposed to happen is that you have a gate and a drawbridge and they operate in unison, that is, as you raise the bridge the gate is lowered and as you lower the bridge the gate is raised. Of course, if you like to be even more ingenious you can arrange that the process goes into reverse ; in any case, I think there is a sporting chance that it will do so ! The number of things that can happen with a project such as this is astounding ! When we tried this at Gilwell we deliberately used spars of about the size of Scout staves, so here again is something which is a fine indoor display item, and it will certainly

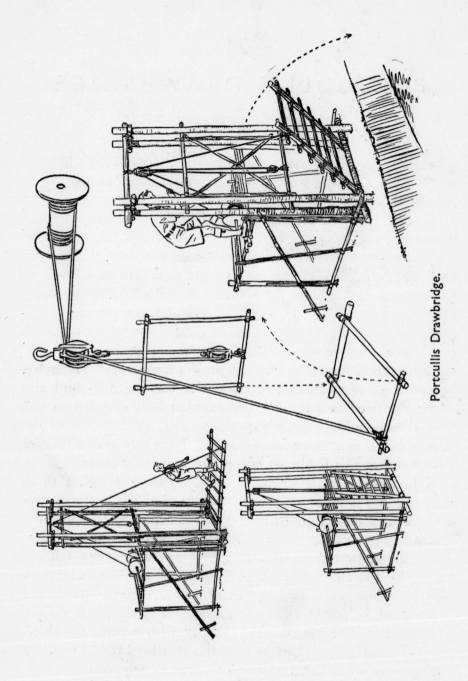

Portcullis Drawbridge.

draw a lot of attention. It might even be incorporated into a pageant if, round the framework, you formed the battlements of a castle, and if it was not so expensive you could also have cauldrons of boiling lead ready to pour down on the opposing forces.

There is one piece of apparatus which you will have to beg or borrow from somewhere, and that is the drum on which the rope winds. It is very easily made but would be difficult to make on the site from rough materials as it needs to run smoothly and the whole has to be dead centre. As you can see from the drawing it is a sort of enormous cotton reel.

The actual roadway can be any length up to but not more than the upright spars. The gate itself should, of course, be the size of the opening it has to cover, and that means that the distance from the ground to the top of the gate must not be more than half the distance between the ground and the top of the structure. Note that the gate is kept in position between two upright spars ; it must have these as guides otherwise it will float about in all directions.

The question of the guys is simply resolved ; if you are building a large project then you may need guy ropes from the top of the upright spars, but in the smaller Scout stave models we have not found it necessary to use guy ropes.

I do hope that a lot of Patrols will have a shot at this, and I hope they will have as much fun putting it into practice as we had in working it out.

25

THE LAZY MAN'S COMMANDO BRIDGE

THOSE of you who have read *Pioneering Projects* will remember that the first project of all is a simple Commando Bridge with two ropes placed one above the other and fastened to trees or stakes in the ground. The idea is that with your feet on the lower rope and your hands on the top rope you simply walk across, and a very fine and easy way it is.

Here I am offering you something rather different : I have called it the Lazy Man's Commando Bridge but, in truth, it requires quite an amount of hard work to erect it and to use it, but the essence of pioneering is to pioneer.

The artist has been a little naughty in the construction of the picture and has forgotten my oft-repeated warning to mask the tree with a bit of old sacking or the tail from the Scoutmaster's shirt. Material put between the rope and the bole of the tree will reduce the wear on the rope and prolong the life of the tree although, admittedly, it contributes nothing to the Scoutmaster's shirt !

You will notice that we show you two methods of using the apparatus ; the artist and I disagree as to which is the best method but we leave it to you as a matter of personal choice. After all, you are the one who will have to decide whether you would rather take the skin off the back of your knees or the inside of your forearm. In the face to the ground method you are unlikely to go to sleep whilst in transit, whilst in the backside to the ground method you might quite literally " drop off ". Note, please in the backside to ground method, " Use for Scout Stave No. 582 " ! Note also, in face to ground method, the ingenious rope-ladder requiring only one rope and the skill of a circus acrobat to climb it.

The Lazy Man's Commando Bridge.

If you have a Troop Headquarters with rafters what a grand Pioneering Relay you can have by using the rope ladder shown in the picture—a ladder for each Patrol—fixed to the beam—up and over—unfastened from the beam—on to the next beam— Patrol up and over, and so on. You wouldn't need much of a programme for the rest of the evening, would you? Making the ladder, explaining the game, getting it started, dealing with the first aid needed, and clearing up afterwards will probably only leave time for " Flag Down " and prayers, but it would be a memorable evening.

Now to return to business. This project is capable of many variations and the one I particularly like is to vary the angle of slope, finding out by experience just how the apparatus can be used in practice. Obviously you can come down at almost any angle but neither the artist nor I are going to show you just what happens if you come down too steeply, and I wonder at what angle the ropes would have to be before you could climb up them? Why not experiment for yourself?

26

THE FLYING TRAPEZE

GEAR REQUIRED

Ropes:
Two 2-inch, 10-foot.
Two 1-inch, 30-foot.

Spars:
Four 15-foot.
Two 7-foot.
One 5-foot.
One 3-foot.

Lashings:
Two 20-foot.
Six 15-foot.

Pickets:
Two.

THIS is very simple to build, the kind of thing a Patrol should be able to erect within an hour but it has the merit not only of simplicity but of being adventurous to use, tremendous fun, and a real muscle builder. The artist has shown it used in two quite different ways, and I want to say a word about each.

In the picture where the sheer legs are actually in the stream the purpose is simply to get from bank to bank or over a small stream or piece of marshy ground, and you will find that it works very well. In the nature of things, not all streams are of that type ; some have the banks almost at water level on one side and much steeper on the other and here, with a little ingenious placing of the structure it is possible to swing from the high bank to the low or from the low to the high. Incidentally, the latter is much easier to do, although to the onlooker it seems more spectacular. It is much easier to land as you are going up, if you can so arrange it.

There is very little to say about the actual structure ; two sheer legs braced with a couple of good ledgers. Obviously you must put on guy ropes, although the artist has left them out so as not to clutter up the drawing with a mass of lines.

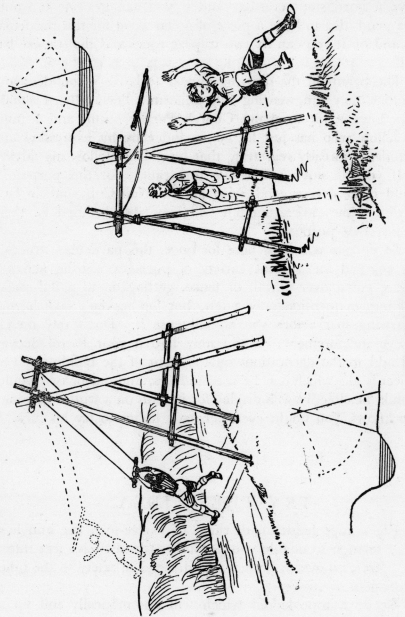

The Flying Trapeze.

Have a good stout crossbar and if you can get one it would be a good idea to have a piece of green wood for this particular job and on it you can fix two trapeze ropes and the trapeze bar itself.

The Scouts in the drawing appear to be very confident and I notice they are wearing full uniform. Personally, I should strip down a bit from my Church Parade outfit, and I think the fellow who has just let go, to judge by his expression and attitude, is already regretting that he did not follow my advice.

If you do not want to use the trapeze for this purpose it would make a very good swing for the Wolf Cubs and, in fact, I think if they are around it will inevitably be used by them for just that purpose.

To end on a serious note for once, this particular structure can be used for a great variety of purposes, getting across a ravine, going over a wall or fence, getting on to a flat-roofed building, to mention only a few, but for heaven's sake have a test swing first before you actually use it. Don't rely merely on eye measurements or you may flatten your Patrol Second and add to the decorations on the front of the building. This project is one which can be used indoors, and one or two would, I think, be effective as a display for parents on a winter evening ; who knows, you might even persuade father to try his luck.

* * * * *

TRY THESE IDEAS

38. Rig a rope ladder with rungs of twelve-inch rise and long enough to enable you to climb at least twelve feet into a tree, go over a branch and descend in safety to the other side.

39. Devise a rope ladder which will automatically roll up as you climb.

27

LAND YACHT

GEAR REQUIRED

Spars:
One 15-foot.
One 10-foot.
Six 5-foot.
Three 3-foot.

Oddments:
One 3-foot plank.
Four wheels.
One 7-foot × 7-foot tarpaulin
or old sheet.

Lashings:
Thirty-six 15-foot.
Six light lines.

I HAVE not really very much to say about this project.

Not all Troops have water available to enable them to build and use rafts, but presumably everybody, except perhaps the Deep Sea Scouts, can get near some land now and then. Where there is land there is often wind, and where there is wind a Land Yacht can be great fun.

The structure is quite obvious from the drawing; you will have to make up two sets of wheels, but surely that is not beyond you. I have not tried it with large wheels; the ones we use are about 12 inches in diameter and they came from war-time paratroopers' trucks. The actual structure is triangular and the mast on which the sail is erected is identical with that on the oil drum raft. The raft is steered from the rear; I know all the modern planes are steered from the front—perhaps we will have a shot at this next time. I think you will find that the steering gear as drawn by the artist is quite practical but obviously you will put another wheel on the other end. Don't try to turn too sharply and don't try too small a boy on this for the first run because it can reach a remarkable speed if there is a wind and the surface is right.

G

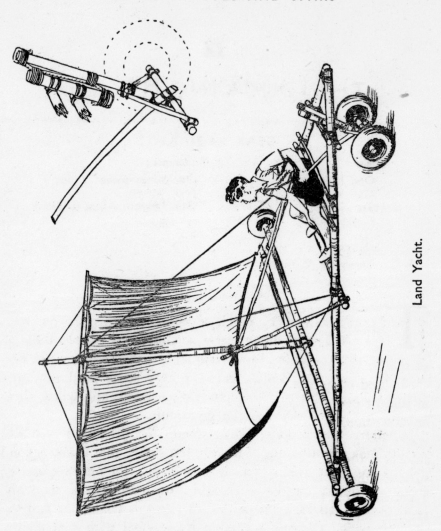

Land Yacht.

The ideal place to use the Land Yacht is the foreshore, on the hard sand after the tide has gone out, but that is not by any means the only place. I am sure you will find endless possibilities and perhaps one of these days we shall have a Land Yacht Race competing with the Soap Box Derby.

28

THE DUCKING STOOL

GEAR REQUIRED

Ropes:
  One 2-inch, 15-foot.

Lashings:
  Twenty-three 15-foot.

Spars:
  One 15-foot.
  One 10-foot.
  Six 5-foot.
  Three 3-foot.

Oddments:
  Seat.

THIS is where my one or two unimaginative friends who always want a good reason for doing a thing are going to sniff a bit, but perhaps they have not got so far as this in the book.

It used to be the custom in England to have a ducking stool in almost every village. It was a fairly cruel business because anyone thought to be a witch was ducked and kept under the water for a considerable length of time. Very often when the stool was brought up the victim had not survived, but if she had survived they proclaimed her as a witch and she was duly burned. I am not, repeat not, recommending this ducking stool for any sadistic purpose, neither do I wish to be accused of reviving medieval tortures or witchcraft and the black arts. This project is offered as a simple bit of fun and in this is its merit. A hot day when in camp, a pleasant pool, and a nice way of cooling the Patrol Leader's fevered brow, that is all there is to it. There is little pioneering skill required but the choice of materials is very important.

The long ducking bar needs to be a fairly stout green wood pole, and it is fixed by a strop lashed to the top of the upright. The V-shaped support is there to take the strain against the

[99]

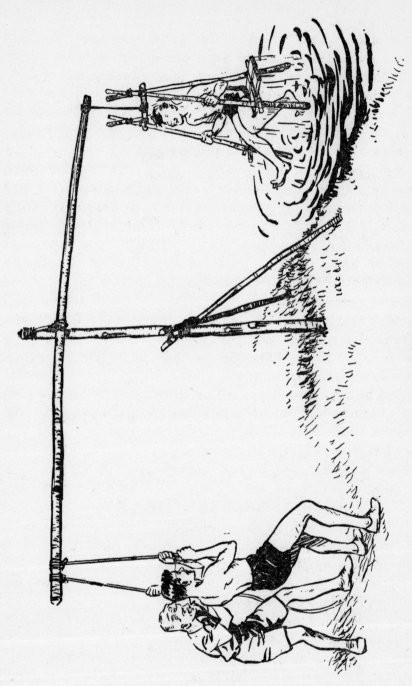

Ducking Stool.

weight of he who is ducked. Of course, you need not make such an elaborate job as the artist has shown, a bosun's chair would do perfectly well and the only reason I asked him to draw it as he did was because sometimes in the bottom of ponds there are old cans and bricks and to be ducked on to them would not be very pleasant; the protruding legs of the stool will provide a safeguard.

One other thing occurs to me about this ducking stool. Perhaps you don't come across them as much today as we used to do, but there always were and still may be boys who funked water. If you are a good swimmer and accustomed to the water it is very hard to understand, but very often these boys were frightened of water because they had never had the opportunity of becoming familiar with it in large quantities. Gently used by a wise Patrol Leader on a nice sunny day the ducking stool might help Tommy the Tenderfoot to overcome the fear he has.

Having shown you the basic idea, cannot you see all the possibilities in this contraption? It can be used as a sort of roundabout and, with a larger crosspiece, as a joisting stand. It would be fun to erect it in the pond with two fellows swinging merrily, armed with mops; at least it would be fun for the spectators.

* * * * *

TRY THESE IDEAS

40. Improvise a gadget for drying firewood and demonstrate it in action.
41. Improvise equipment to deal with a casualty who has fallen through ice, the hole being at least twelve feet from solid ground.

29

PHEW!!!

ALL right, let's begin by agreeing that it's ridiculous and that there are more profitable ways of spending an hour than building this thing, that it will probably be very difficult and may not work when it is finished. Having agreed all that I still hope somebody will have sufficient spirit of fun to have a go at it.

The requirements are obvious : A spirit of adventure, one not too precious bicycle, a few spars and drums and various bits and pieces for the rudder as shown in the drawing. The intention, for what it is worth, is that having fixed a simple paddle in place on the rear wheel of the bicycle you simply pedal your way across the pond or the river. I am intrigued by the buffers at the front ! The rudder is of impeccable design and could not possibly go wrong, always provided that you keep the boat moving. (I think " boat " is rather a stretch of the imagination and we had better just call it The Thing.)

The Senior Scout De Luxe Model uses the auto-cycle technique instead of the more mundane method of pedalling but it has the great advantage that if you begin to flounder you have oil to calm the waters and petrol to light as signal flares !

I want to be quite frank with you. We have not had time to try this out in practice and it is the only idea in the book which has not been tried. It is an idea about which I talked to the artist and I think he has done a magnificent job but, when you have got over the shock, will you try to make this gadget or something like it and let me know what you think about it ? Be as rude as you like, but do be practical and tell me what is wrong with the idea and how you think it can be made to work. It really would be a great day if we could see a British Contingent arriving at a Jamboree mounted on these things !

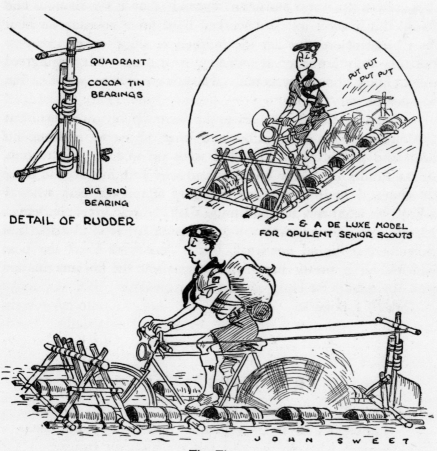

DETAIL OF RUDDER

QUADRANT

COCOA TIN BEARINGS

BIG END BEARING

PUT PUT PUT PUT

— & A DE LUXE MODEL FOR OPULENT SENIOR SCOUTS

JOHN SWEET

The Thing.

All this reminds me of a true story which I think is worth recording.

A few years ago, running a Training Course at Gilwell, I asked a Patrol to make one of the Paddle Steamer Rafts shown in *Pioneering Projects* ; I think it was Mark II, that is, the one with the paddles port and starboard instead of over the stern. The Patrol did a good job and worked hard for a couple of hours. As a piece of creative art the finished product looked dreadful but they duly launched it and four men boarded it, their total weight being about fifty stones. There happened to be a German Scouter on the Course, a very pleasant quiet chap. I noticed him watching this Paddle Steamer Raft moving in a drunken fashion across the Bomb Hole and when he began nodding his head and muttering to himself I went up to him ; he turned, smiled, and said, ' Now I understand why Britain won the war.' Of course I hadn't expected that sort of remark, and when I asked him what this raft had to do with the war his reply, which I shall never forget, was this : ' This thing, it is absurd, it is ridiculous, it should not work, but it does work ! ' I think he had hit on a pretty big truth. Certainly the project in this picture qualifies for being absurd and ridiculous : Will you make it work ? I hope so !

*   *   *   *   *

TRY THESE IDEAS

42. Assuming that your Patrol Leader has been stricken by lumbago and is consequently unable to bend, make a gadget whereby he can put on his own trousers whilst remaining in an upright position.

43. Using a cart wheel or something similar as a base, pitch a hike tent on a turntable so that your tent can always back the wind. The next stage, of course, is to rig simple sails so that this happens automatically.

FRENCH SCOUTS TRAINING AS TRAPEZE ARTISTS

GANTRY

PYRAMID TOWER

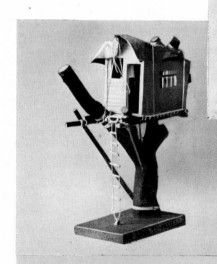

DOUBLE   SWING BRIDGE

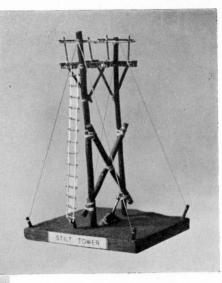

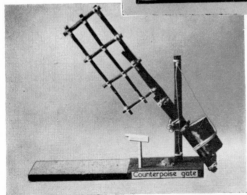

INDOOR PIONEERING

30

COOLING THE FEVERED BROW

LET me begin by admitting quite freely and frankly that there are easier ways of getting a bucket of water thrown over your head and shoulders. Those of you who have read with me through the years will know that I am never concerned with finding the easiest way but always with the most interesting way and one which will put into practice some of the things we teach Scouts.

The gadget shown is simple enough ; two pairs of sheer legs properly braced and a simple runway with a nice little trip bar to catch the full bucket as it arrives at its destination. This might almost have been borrowed from the Spanish Inquisition and certainly on a winter day it would require considerable courage to stand there whilst a bucket full of icy water emptied itself on to your head. If you do perform this trick in the winter my advice is to make sure that it is icy water and not a solid block of ice which descends upon your head.

Several times in this book I have suggested that you should encourage your Scouts to make their own " bill of quantities ". In the first book on pioneering I did it for you but I think it is excellent training for the Scouts to say exactly what is required for any particular project, and I hope you will get them doing it.

I hope also you will take a project like this and experiment with it, adapt it, and improve it. For example, it should not be difficult to make the bucket fill itself. Perhaps you could get the hold-fast into the stream so that the bucket would fall directly into the water, in which case a Scout could work the whole apparatus single-handed. It could be used without the trip bar as a " Lazy Man's Method of Obtaining Washing up Water ". In fact, you could almost have the washing up done in running water.

I rate this particular project as an elementary one which I

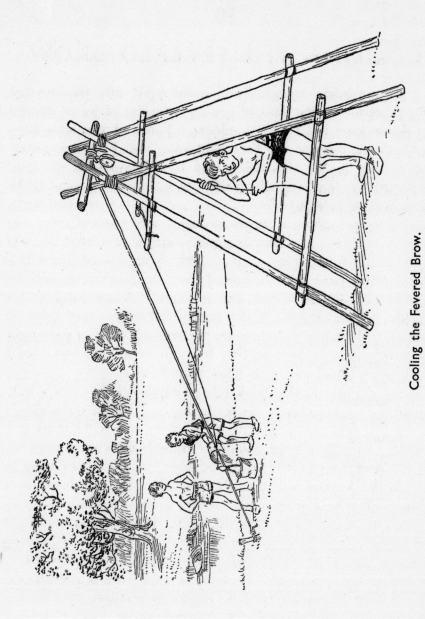

Cooling the Fevered Brow.

should let a Patrol tackle as soon as I was satisfied that they could do a square lashing and a sheer lashing and when they knew how to mouse a hook.

It is interesting to look at this drawing and to realise that the only knot a Scout needs to know how to make is the Clove Hitch. As a matter of fact, the longer I play about with pioneering the more I believe that the only two essential knots are the Clove Hitch and the Sheet Bend. I like to learn others and I like teaching them to other people, but I am prepared to make almost everything in this book on the basis of these two knots.

Finally, to save you writing and asking why the Scout under the shower is wearing his shoes I would inform you that he is doing so in order to run faster if his courage fails !

* * * * *

TRY THESE IDEAS

44. Using a conveyor belt principle try to devise a system for speeding the washing up in camp.
45. Make a remote control and entirely safe hurricane lamp turner-outer.
46. Design and make a top boot remover capable of being operated :
    (*a*) By the wearer of the boots.
    (*b*) By a Scout who wishes to help but who must remain out of range during the operation.
47. Design and make a commissioner catcher. (Care must be taken that no harm befalls the specimen thus captured, who must be kept in good condition and in reasonable comfort.)
48. Design and construct a device for making water run up hill.

31

AERIAL RUNWAY BRAKE

IN *Pioneering Projects* I gave you a design for an Aerial Runway which, incidentally, my Australian friends call " The Flying Fox ". The gadget I want to talk about now, which we have illustrated for you, is a fairly recent invention which I think has much to commend it.

One of the snags of the Aerial Runway is that if the angle of descent is too steep you are faced with the delightful alternatives of breaking your legs, bruising your spine, or flattening your nose on the sheer legs. There is no reliable method of stopping yourself and yet a good brake is essential to any vehicle and I suppose you could call a Bosun's Chair a vehicle without stretching the imagination too far.

If you look at Figure 1 you will notice that fixed on to the eye of the main carrying block is a similar smaller block which is running free on a rope that is fixed above the highest point of the main runway rope. This secondary rope ought to be about one and a half times the length of the runway. You must have a trusted friend and I use the words very deliberately—yes, a trusted friend at the sheer legs end of the runway, holding on to the secondary rope. Figure 2 shows what he has to do in order to apply the brake. At the moment when he thinks your ride should be brought to a halt he takes two or three paces to the left or, if he prefers it, to the right, so that he places himself at an angle to the line of descent. We have found that even at quite high speeds the braking effect is immediate and, providing the passenger is holding on firmly, he is stopped in his mad career. If, of course, he is riding " no hands " he is liable to be jerked out of the contraption, which is not noticeably better than flattening one's nose.

Another problem about the Aerial Runway is " How do you get on to the darn thing to start with ? " In the previous book

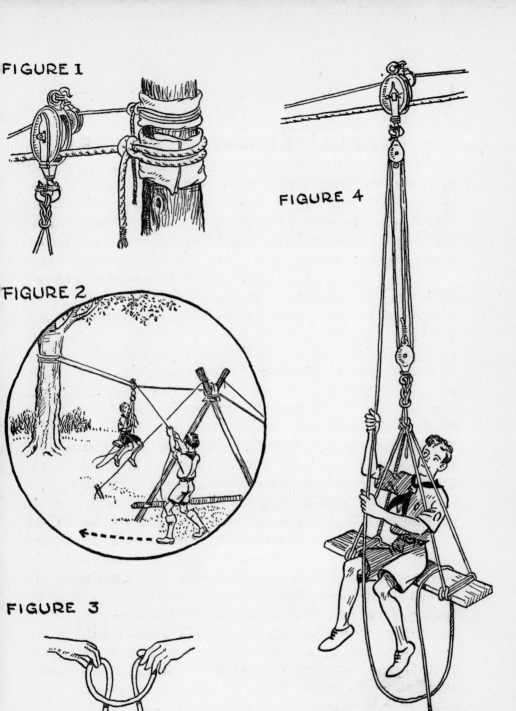

FIGURE 1

FIGURE 2

FIGURE 3

FIGURE 4

Aerial Runway Brake.

[109]

I showed a rope ladder and platform, and that is obviously a good way but it needs more equipment and takes more time and is not quite so exciting as pulling yourself up.

Figure 3 shows you how to make a Catspaw, which is the neatest way of fixing the Bosun's Chair ropes on to the hoist. With the two to one pulley—and note that the " two " is at the top and the " one " at the bottom—it is quite possible to hoist yourself up. Incidentally, it is important to advise the Scout concerned to go on holding himself up when he is there, but the advice is usually only needed once ! Another advantage of this arrangement is that more people can use the runway and there is far less delay in getting the chair back into place and the next man on. I have seen the whole affair run almost as a relay race but I still hope to see four Patrols of a Troop running a relay race on four separate runways.

I would like you to look at Figure 4 again as although the artist tried hard it is not easy to make everything quite clear. The best and undoubtedly the safest way of making a Bosun's Chair is to use only one rope. The artist has shown you a Scaffold Hitch at each end of the plank and the rope fastened to the hook, as I have already explained, using a catspaw. The hook is moused and unless you have chosen a singularly poor rope there should be no danger involved.

I do hope that you will not think either the Bosun's Chair or the Brake are too elaborate. It is true that they involve a little more equipment but they are worth while from every point of view. The first time I saw the brake in action I was really excited about it and when I sat on the chair and went down the runway I was even more excited to find how well it worked.

Finally : credit where it belongs. The braking device was invented by Ian Graham and I hope you will call it Graham's Braking Device, because that is what I shall certainly be calling it.

32

THE PILE DRIVER

ERE is a piece of unnecessary nonsense : I am not even convinced that it will work and I must admit that I have not tried it out in action. This is one occasion when I gave the artist his head, with the astonishing results that you see.

You will, of course, have realised long since that there are more purposes in this book than just being practical. I have no desire to stop anyone having a shot at any form of pioneering that they may find amusing and, from a training point of view, a great deal can be learned by trying out something of this nature as it at least gives practice in lashing and shows the limitations of the various types of blocks and tackle. When you realise that nearly all the great discoveries of the world have been made by amateurs, who knows but that we might, between us, unearth a new idea ?

I must admit, however, that there are easier ways of putting a picket into the ground and the method demonstrated is not by any means the best, but I hope that will not prevent you, on some summer evening when you are at a loss for an idea, pulling this out of the archives and offering it to a Patrol.

Knowing the artist as I do I think the whole conception owes something to the guillotine ; all he has really done is to replace the knife with a lump of wood, the ultimate effect of which upon a shaven neck would be identical with the French method of old.

Quite apart from the constructional skill needed, in this particular piece of nonsense there is something involved that we have not done before, that is, the making of a rope ring or grommet, in my view one of the most difficult pieces of splicing for the simple reason that when making a successful grommet the rope gets increasingly tight and each successive tuck is accordingly more difficult and requires more strength.

Well, there it is. I hope you will try it and I hope you will find other uses for the principle involved. At random I can

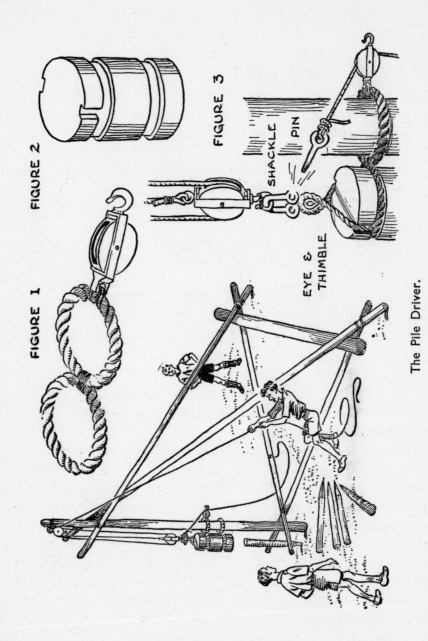

FIGURE 1

FIGURE 2

FIGURE 3

SHACKLE

PIN

EYE &
THIMBLE

The Pile Driver.

suggest a trap for the unwary, a method of creating a mighty splash in a pond, a means of persuading an unruly Troop Leader that his Scoutmaster's ideas are worthy of admission to his thick skull and, lastly, an eminently practical suggestion, what about trying it as a potato masher, a clothes wringer, or a rissole maker ?

*   *   *   *   *

TRY THESE IDEAS

49. It is generally accepted that a tent peg should be driven into the ground at right angles to the guy line. Conduct a series of experiments varying the angle and try to rig some mechanical gadget to prove or disprove the opening sentence.
50. Build an apparatus to carry written messages in either direction between the Patrol tent and the Patrol kitchen.

33

ROPE TACKLE OR HAYMAN'S HITCH — REEVING A TACKLE — AN ANCHORAGE PROBLEM

Rope Tackle or Hayman's Hitch

THIS is an excellent method of getting a rough and ready two to one purchase when there are no blocks available. It is very simple to tie, being in effect half a Sheep Shank. Its chief disadvantage is the tremendous wear on the rope. If, for example, you are using this method to strain a new rope then it is better to make the Hayman's Hitch in an old rope, attaching it with a Sheet Bend to the new rope and not putting the wear on the new rope.

Reeving a Tackle

IDEALLY, as the artist shows, this is a two-man job, especially if the rope is at all heavy. Note carefully that the eyes of the blocks point inwards, that is, towards each other, and the hooks point away from each other or outwards.

The most normal make-up for a block and tackle is a block with two sheaves at one end and a block with one sheave at the other end. The reeving of the tackle starts by the man with the two sheave block, working from right to left, passing the line to the second man who likewise works from right to left and then passes the line back to the first man so that it can go through his second sheave, still from right to left, with the second man fastening off through the eye of the smaller block. I am afraid all too few Scouts are given the opportunity of reeving blocks and tackle : I find that Scouters tend to make these up, quite adequately as a rule, and then put them into store. I think that somewhere

ROPE TACKLE OR HAYMAN'S HITCH

WHEN NO BLOCKS ARE AVAILABLE THIS USEFUL DEVICE GIVES A ROUGH-&-READY TWO-ONE PURCHASE. IT IS MERELY A HALF-MADE SHEEPSHANK WITH THE FREE END PASSED ROUND A TREE & DOUBLED BACK THROUGH THE BIGHT

REEVING A TACKLE

TWO MEN STAND BACK TO BACK WITH BLOCKS IN FRONT, HOOKS POINTING AWAY & ROPE ON RIGHT OF MAN WITH BLOCK HAVING MOST SHEAVES. THE ROPE IS PASSED THROUGH LOWER SHEAVE FROM RIGHT TO LEFT & THEN THROUGH LOWER SHEAVE OF SECOND BLOCK, & SO ON TILL THE TACKLE IS MADE UP BY TYING OFF TO EYE OF SECOND BLOCK

ONE MAN CAN HOLD A CONSIDERABLE STRAIN OR THE "STOPPER" CAN BE WHIPPED TO THE HAWSER WITH SISAL

HALF HITCH <u>ACROSS</u> THE LAY

TURNS <u>WITH</u> THE LAY

PASSING A STOPPER

TO TRANSFER A HAWSER FROM A FAULTY ANCHORAGE WHILE MAINTAINING THE STRAIN; A TEMPORARY "STOPPER" IS APPLIED. THE FREE END OF THE HAWSER MAY THEN BE UNHITCHED & TRANSFERRED TO THE NEW PICKET.

between Second and First Class every Scout ought to have the chance of reeving his own blocks. It is one of those things which looks easy but unless you are trained to do it properly there are many places where you can go wrong. For example, you can start with the wrong block, get the ropes crossed, change direction and, in fact, make the whole thing unusable. Yes, I would like every Scout to be able to do this job. I know it is not in the tests, but what of that?

An Anchorage Problem

ANYONE who has done even a small amount of pioneering has probably been faced with the situation envisaged here. With the greatest care in the world something goes wrong and one of the anchorages begins to give. Obviously, we do not want to dismantle the whole job but we do need to transfer the load from the faulty anchorage to a new and secure one. Generally speaking, it is much wiser to handle it this way rather than to strengthen the weak anchorage.

I think what the artist has drawn is perfectly clear. The important thing to remember is to immediately take the strain from the weakened anchorage, then prepare the new anchorage, and finally transfer the weight to the new anchorage.

* * * * *

TRY THIS IDEA

51. Make a mat from natural materials to go beside the P.L.'s bed.

34

REMOVING A STUBBORN PICKET— CARRYING FIREWOOD — RAISING A LOAD, USING MAKESHIFT TACKLE

Removing a Stubborn Picket

THIS is a familiar problem and the reverse of the previous one. Here we have a picket that is difficult to remove after the bridge has been dismantled. This is a constant problem at Gilwell where the soil is heavy, clinging clay and, in fact, one sometimes feels that Old Nick himself is hanging on to the other end of the picket, holding on grimly and refusing to be drawn to the surface.

The artist shows us a method of using a lever spar, which really is as effective as any method we have discovered and much better than trying to loosen the picket by knocking it sideways : Along that road lie many smashed pickets and not a few frayed tempers.

I would slightly criticise the drawing in that the lever spar ought to be thicker than the picket we are trying to draw out. The spar will have a substantial strain put upon it and it needs to be stronger than something a Scout can break over a fulcrum. However, experience is the best teacher and there is not much use in trying to produce a formula.

Carrying Firewood

HERE is a useful dodge which I can thoroughly commend to you. There are few more awkward things to carry than a bundle of sticks. In some circumstances you can drag them over the ground but they are liable to become caught on every knob or stone and it really is easier to carry the bundle.

[117]

USING A HEAD-STRAP
TO CARRY A WEIGHT

RAISING A LOAD
WITH A
MAKESHIFT TACKLE

APPLYING A LEVER SPAR
TO DRAW A PICKET

THE INDIAN TRAVOIS

A number of native races make use of the head strap, and this is something every Scout should try out for himself. I suggest you get your Scouts to practise with quite light loads and gradually find out the weight they can comfortably and safely carry.

If the head strap does not appeal to you then what about our next sketch : **The Indian Travois.** This is no more than a pair of sheer legs with a few lashings across the wider end. On reasonably even ground quite a young Scout can move a heavy load without any strain. The kind of thing I find we often need to move is, for example, a heavy tent from the lorry that brought it and, judging by some I see, the Scoutmaster's personal kit might come into the same category.

Raising a Load, Using Makeshift Tackle

THERE is really nothing to say about this as the drawing shows you all that is necessary, but it is a useful dodge and I think Scouts should be shown how to use it. The Parbuckling system could be used also, but the point I wish to make is that the more variety we bring into pioneering the more interesting it becomes.

* * * * *

TRY THIS IDEA

52. Construct a pair of elevated soles to attach to normal shoes so that the wearer is at least six inches off the ground. There is no sense in this unless the wearer can walk in the shoes !

35

TOPPING A TREE WITH A CHAIN SAW — THE "PLOUGH" TRACKMAKER — PORTABLE WIND-BREAK — CAMP TABLE

Topping a Tree with a Chain Saw

I HOPE you have a chain saw in your Troop equipment ; I think it is one of the most useful and interesting pieces of pioneering equipment that has ever been devised. The chain saw is very light and portable and it can be used in almost any situation.

The artist has shown you a very good dodge for topping a tree, using a couple of blocks to keep the saw at the angle required. The two Scouts working on the job are at a safe distance from the tree and you will notice that the saw is giving a good clean cut where it is wanted.

Tree topping without a chain saw is beyond the capacity of most Scouts for the simple reason that once you have climbed the tree—and in some circumstances that is easier said than done —there is no room to work and it is an effort to hold on and preserve one's balance, so that there is no strength left to use either an axe or a saw.

A few months ago I asked a Crew of six Rovers to top a lime tree at Gilwell, thirty feet above the ground. They were all experienced and they worked very hard but without a chain saw it took them a whole day to top the tree which was only about 15 inches in diameter.

We use chain saws a great deal at Gilwell because we have to do a lot of topping of dead timber. Sometimes we use a ladder to get into the tree but one way I commend to you, which I do not pretend is easy but good fun, is to use a bow and arrow to shoot

THE "PLOUGH" TRACKMAKER

PORTABLE WINDBREAK

TOPPING A TREE WITH
THE CHAIN SAW

A CAMP TABLE

a light line over the bough it is intended to cut. Attach a rope to the line and the other end of the rope to the chain saw, draw it up into the tree and attach a rope to the other end of the saw before drawing it up. In this way the chain saw can be used at a good height without anyone having to climb the tree.

The "Plough" Trackmaker

THE drawing the artist shows requires very little explanation. This is a two-man job in operation, and this I do commend to you.

The actual construction of the important part is simple : Take a half log which is fairly heavy and stud it with nails and spikes so that it will leave a distinct trail even on ground that is otherwise a little dubious about accepting tracks.

It might be an idea for every Patrol to make a Trackmaker of its own and to give it a special pattern so that any Scout in the Troop will know without question which Patrol had laid the trail. It is this kind of development that I believe helps the Patrol spirit a great deal. The Scouters might also have their own model.

One word of warning : A thing of this nature is fine on rough ground but not the kind of thing to use on a public footpath or across a newly-rolled gravel path.

Portable Windbreak

THIS can be a useful gadget, especially on an exposed camp site. The artist shows a Scout using it for a quiet rest but this is the sort of thing I think can well be used on an exposed site outside the tent door. I have no use at all for people who sleep with tent doors shut. It seems to me quite fatuous to go out into the open air and then build up a fug which is probably much more potent than any we would have in our own bedrooms. On the other hand, it is difficult to sleep when the wind is howling through the tent. The wind break provides the right answer as the wind can get into the tent but cannot rush in.

You might like a wind break as part of the kitchen equipment at Summer Camp, so that the cooks can work in comfort on a windy day and the fire can be controlled.

The same design, which is easy enough to make up on the site if the materials are available, will make an excellent screen for latrines or the grease pit.

Hazel, chestnut, and willow are the best woods in Great Britain for this sort of thing, but any whippy twigs can be pressed into service.

One query I have about the artist's effort is that if the Scout is really sheltering from the wind then surely the guy lines are on the wrong side. Personally, I would play safe and have the guy lines running each way.

Camp Table

THIS is a pleasant idea for a Patrol. There is no problem in the construction and it has the great advantage that it really is a table which can be laid and made to look attractive. There is a convenient shelf higher up, possibly for the second course, and in a sudden shower of rain it would be easy to throw a tarpaulin or a tent flysheet over the top of the sheer legs and provide reasonable shelter. For the athletically inclined, after the table has been cleared, what better than a little digestion-restoring trapeze work?

* * * * *

TRY THIS IDEA

53. Mechanise the washing-up in the kitchen. If you use an old bicycle as the motive power and a conveyor belt system you ought at least to get a mop moving round a dixie, a scrubbing brush to operate, and a device for tipping dirty water into a hole.

36

THE BODGER'S LATHE — THE CAMP LOOM

The Bodger's Lathe

THIS used to be very popular in Scouting but I have not seen one in action for many years. They really do work and next time you are in camp with an idle hour make it less idle by making one of these gadgets and fashioning a little camp furniture.

The principle is obvious enough ; the main part of the apparatus is the whippy, overhead stick. An Ash sapling is probably the best but Willow will do quite well. You can, with experience, work at high speed and I have seen beautiful camp candlesticks, legs of stools, etc., made by Scouts on a Bodger's lathe they have constructed themselves.

The Camp Loom

I AM one who has never had a lot of faith in the hip hole. I must confess that, after many years camping, I have a great liking for something comfortable between me and the ground.

The camp loom will make a first-class mattress from hay or straw and it is good fun to use. The drawing shows the principle. You will notice that it is manned by three Scouts, which is the ideal number, and perhaps two more could bring reserves of material. Hay is the best material but bracken will do almost as well and even—and it may surprise you—tops of Spruce or Yew trees that have been recently felled.

BODGER'S LATHE

CAMP LOOM

SNOWSHOES

"THE SNOWBALLISTA"

37

SNOW SHOES — THE SNOW BALLISTA

Snow Shoes

AND why not? These are useful articles and if the snow melts we can use them as broilers. There is nothing remarkable about the design and those we show here are made from green sticks of about half an inch in diameter.

The Snow Ballista

YOU may be surprised to learn that recently at Gilwell we had officers of the Royal Air Force enthusiastically making this sort of apparatus. They were not here when the snow was on the ground but we found we could throw cricket balls a fair distance by using the ballista, although not always in the expected direction.

There is little lashing involved. For the best results the whole Patrol needs to get on the starting apparatus and they will be able to work up a tremendous speed and the snow ball or cricket ball, in theory at least, will fly off with an astonishing muzzle velocity.